Our Boys
and
The Wise Men

The Origins of Dundee Football Club

James K. Corstorphine

Text Copyright © 2020 James K. Corstorphine

All rights reserved

ISBN: 9798643521549

No part of this publication may be reproduced, stored in a retrieval system or transmitted in any form or by any means without the prior permission of the publisher.

Front Cover: Victorian etching of a late Nineteenth Century football scene.

Other Publications by James K. Corstorphine:

East of Thornton Junction: The Story of the FifeCoast Line
(James K. Corstorphine, 1995). ISBN: 9781976909283

Peter Smith, the Fisherman Poet of Cellardyke
(James K. Corstorphine / Peter Smith Snr., 2000) ISBN: 0-9525621-2-X

On That Windswept Plain: The First One Hundred Years of East Fife Football Club
(James K. Corstorphine, 2003). ISBN: 9781976888618

The Earliest Fife Football Clubs
(James K. Corstorphine, 2018) ISBN: 9781980249580

Dyker Lad: Recollections of Life in an East Neuk of FifeFishingVillage
(Alexander 'Sonny' Corstorphine, 2018) ISBN: 9781981019137

All of the above titles are also available in Kindle eBook format

Contents

	Page
Introduction	5
Chapter One: Dundee's First Association Football Club	9
Chapter Two: The Formation of East End	17
Chapter Three: Our Boys Enter the Fray	21
Chapter Four: Early Days	27
Chapter Five: An Intense Rivalry Starts to Build	37
Chapter Six: The Forfarshire Football Association	49
Chapter Seven: The Burns Charity Cup	61
Chapter Eight: A Hooligan Element Starts to Creep In	71
Chapter Nine: Football Fever	83
Chapter Ten: Contrasting Fortunes	95
Chapter Eleven: The Forfarshire Clubs Make Their Mark	103
Chapter Twelve: More Battles and More Bickering	115
Chapter Thirteen: The Re-emergence of East End	127
Chapter Fourteen: Our Boys Win 'The Double'	141
Chapter Fifteen: The Northern League	153
Chapter Sixteen: The Lure of Professionalism	167
Chapter Seventeen: The Merger of Our Boys and East End	177
Epilogue	187
Sources and Bibliography	191

Introduction

The history of football clubs founded in the nineteenth century is a fascinating subject. As the popularity of Association football spread from the west of Scotland through to the east during the 1870's, several Association clubs were founded in the Dundee area. The game of football had, of course, been played in various formats in and around Dundee long before the arrival of the Association game, and its local origins are lost in the mists of time.

The earliest documented evidence that can be found relating to football in Dundee appeared in the Dundee Courier in 1861, contained within a report on a meeting of Dundee Town Council, held on Wednesday 17th April. The article reported that a letter had been submitted to the council by a group of young men going by the name of the 'Early Rising Club', who wished to lodge a complaint that they had been prevented from playing football in BarrackPark between the hours of six and eight on the previous Friday morning. The group had been of the opinion that football was an *"innocent amusement"*, and that they were doing no harm.

The council disagreed, however, and in closing the matter commented that: *"It would never do to have a dozen or two young men running through the park after a football"*, before adding: *"such games might be dangerous to parties frequenting the park"*.

A few miles further east, in Broughty Ferry, the game was also gaining popularity during the 1860's, especially with the younger generation. Again, just like in Dundee, the pastime was not to everyone's liking, and one local resident, incensed with young footballers regularly kicking their ball into his garden, was reported to have driven his pitchfork through the ball on one occasion before the boys had managed to recover it from his property.

This action was to land the gentleman in trouble, however, as one of the boys' parents successfully sued for replacement of the ball, at a cost of twenty-one shillings (£1.05) plus legal costs!

Despite these early reports on how football was regarded by many to be more of a nuisance than an innocent pastime, it was inevitable that Association football would eventually become established in the local area as 'football fever' swept through the country.

On New Year's Day 1876, the first recorded Association football match in Dundee was played in BaxterPark between the Burgh's first Association club, St. Clement's, and Glasgow side Alexandra Athletic. The local side lost this inaugural encounter heavily by five-goals-to-one, but even a defeat of this magnitude did little to dampen the local footballers' enthusiasm.

Within a few years, several other Association clubs had been founded in and around Dundee, and the game was destined to go from strength to strength as its popularity grew in line with a huge increase in the local population brought about by the influx of thousands of workers lured to the local area to work in the jute mills.

Two of the earliest Association football clubs in Dundee were East End, founded in 1877; and Our Boys, founded just over a year later during the summer of 1878. Incidentally, some sources claim that Our Boys were also founded in 1877, but in all probability this confusion arises from the fact that a Glasgow team of the same name competed in the Scottish Cup in September of that year.

Several years later, in 1893, these two clubs were to amalgamate to form Dundee Football Club, destined to become established in future years as one of Scotland's most respected sides.

There were a number of reasons behind the amalgamation of Our Boys and East End, but the main thinking behind the merger was that both clubs felt the time was right for Dundee to have a professional side capable of competing in the Scottish Football League, which had been founded just three years earlier.

Professionalism had been sweeping through the game of Association football in England following the legalisation of monetary payment to players in 1885. In the years leading up to the formation of Dundee F.C. eight years later, local teams had been losing players to clubs from south of the border, and in some cases almost their entire team had ventured south in order to earn a wage from playing the game.

In May 1893, the Scottish Football Association finally bowed to the inevitable, and sanctioned the introduction of professionalism in Scotland. Realising that they now had the means to stem the flow of local football talent from Dundee and the local area, East End and Our Boys wasted no time in joining forces and, just a few weeks after professionalism had been introduced to the Scottish game, Dundee Football Club was born.

This book details the history of East End and Our Boys football clubs, as well as briefly illustrating the history and background of some of the other influential teams that operated in Dundee and the surrounding area during the late nineteenth century.

THE DOOLEY FITBA' CLUB

Written by JAMES CURRIN

Noo ye a' ken my big brither Jock,
His richt name is Johnny Shaw,
Well he's lately jined a fitba club,
For he's daft aboot fitba';
He's twa black een already an
Three teeth oot by the root,
Whaur his face did come in contact wi'
Some ither fellow's boot.

Chorus:
He's fitba' crazy fegs,
He's clean stane mad,
His fitba' capers robbed him o'
Whit we bit sense he had;
It wid tak a dizen servents
His claes tae patch and scrub,
Since Jock's become a member o'
the Dooley fitba' club.

Noo the first match they ever played,
I went mysel' and saw,
they'd twa half bricks for goal-posts
an' a tin can for a ba';
The Prince o' Wales was present an'
Some lords and ladies grand,
So our Jock he got an egg box an'
erected a grand stand.

The auld wife sweers she'll put him oot
That's if he disna' keep
Frae kickin' up a rumpus
Playin' fitba, through his sleep;
He'll cry oot it's a corner kick,
Or something else sae droll,
'Thither nicht he kicked me oot o' bed
And he swore it was a goal.

"The Dooley Fitba' Club", widely regarded as the first-ever football song, was written in the 1880's by Glasgow songwriter James Curran. 'Dooley' is simply an old Scots word for 'Dopey'.

1

Dundee's First Association Football Club

Dundee's first Association football club, St. Clement's, were founded in late 1875, just a matter of weeks before the district's first-ever Association football match was played in Baxter Park on New Year's Day 1876 between St. Clement's and Glasgow club Alexandra Athletic, which the visitors won by five-goals-to-one.

Undaunted, St. Clement's wasted little time in arranging a follow-up game and, just a few weeks later, the second eleven of the famous Glasgow club Queen's Park visited Baxter Park on Saturday 15th February 1876. Reporting on the match, which the visitors won by three-goals-to-nil, the Dundee Courier were of the opinion that the local players had given a good account of themselves despite the score-line, and stated that:

"The home team, by some good play, endeavoured several times to storm their opponents' goal, and once or twice succeeded in carrying it to within a few yards of the posts, but the combined play of the strangers always seemed to keep their goal safe."

The report also hinted that most, if not all, of the St. Clement's players were more accustomed to following the Rugby code, as several free-kicks had been conceded throughout the game due to the players handling the ball un-necessarily:

"A great advantage the Glasgow team had over their Dundee brethren was the number of free kicks they obtained by the latter frequently handling the ball, they, seemingly, not having quite forgotten the Rugby rules before commencing to learn those used in the Association game."

The report on that particular match concluded with the rather intriguing opinion that Association football was a welcome respite from *"all that is objectionable"* in the rougher game of Rugby!

The friendly association between St. Clement's and Queen's Park continued for the remainder of the season, but that camaraderie was put to the test when the Dundee club failed to show up for a match scheduled for Hampden Park on Thursday 13th April. With the Queen's Park team stripped and ready for action, the Glasgow men awaited the arrival of the side from Dundee in vain. After waiting on the park for over an hour, it became obvious that the game would not be taking place, and the players and assembled spectators headed for home.

It later transpired that St. Clement's had telegraphed the Glasgow club on the previous evening stating that they could not muster their whole team, to which Queen's Park had replied that they could provide players to fill the vacant positions in the Dundee side. It would appear that the latter message was never received.

Just over two weeks later, however, on Saturday 29th April, the match did eventually go ahead in Glasgow. Despite losing again, this time by three-goals-to-one, St. Clement's gave a good account of themselves; scoring a goal which, according to the subsequent match report: *"was well merited, and was loudly cheered by the spectators"*.

By all accounts, St. Clement's had matched their more illustrious opponents in every department, especially during the second half, and expectations were high for the future of the recently-founded Dundee side.

The following season, St. Clement's considered themselves worthy of competing in the Scottish Cup, and duly entered the country's premier football competition.

The Dundee side was subsequently drawn to face 3rd Edinburgh Rifle Volunteers in the first round, with the match scheduled to be played in Kirkcaldy on Saturday 30th September 1876.

The reason for playing the match in Fife is unclear. It is possible, however, that Kirkcaldy's Newton Park, then an established sports ground, was considered to be a more suitable venue than Dundee's Baxter Park or Magdalen Green as it was situated close to the main railway line between Dundee and Edinburgh, therefore making it more accessible to followers of both sides. Kirkcaldy is also equidistant from Dundee and Edinburgh.

St. Clement's won their first-ever competitive match by a single goal, scored early in the first half by forward J. Striven, which earned the Dundee side a second round meeting with another Edinburgh team, St. Andrew's.

Again, NewtonPark was the preferred venue for the cup-tie. Although St Clement's played the better football during the first-half, the game remained goal-less until a second-half own-goal broke the deadlock and put the Edinburgh side in front. Going behind under such unfortunate circumstances simply spurred the Dundee side on, however, and the game was turned around thanks to goals from Sharp and McLennan. *"The spectators were treated to an excellent exhibition of the game"* reported the Dundee Courier, who also observed that: *"play became fast and exciting, the ball being taken merrily from goal to goal"*.

By beating St Andrew's, St. Clement's became one of just twenty clubs remaining in that season's Scottish Cup competition.

In the third round, St. Clement's were drawn to face Glasgow club Northern, at home, and this time the match was actually played in Dundee, at Magdalen Green, on Saturday 11th November 1876.

With the playing surface under six or seven inches of snow, however, the match was a disappointing one as far as skilful play was concerned.

To make matters even more difficult, St. Clement's were without the services of club captain McLennan, which had *"considerably weakened"* the team according to the local press. Consequently, the Dundee side exited the competition following defeat by two-goals-to-one.

Association football was by now growing rapidly in popularity in the local area; and, before the end of the 1876/77 season, St. Clement's had included on their fixture list matches against newly-formed Dundee club Dunmore, as well as Abertay, a rugby team from Broughty Ferry. The latter named side was actually just one of many rugby clubs experimenting with the Association game at that time!

The following season saw St Clement's enter the Scottish Cup for a second time, which drew the following comments from the Dundee Evening Telegraph on Monday 29th October 1877:

"During the past two or three years the game of football, as played according to Association rules, has spread over a very wide area. This increase is doubtless due to many causes, and perhaps not the least of these has been the liberality of the Scottish Football Association, which presented a handsome challenge cup to be competed for annually by those clubs playing the rules of, and enrolled in, the Association. The ties are drawn in districts, the first this quarter being between the St Clement, local Club, and the Dunfermline, of Dunfermline. Dunfermline, however, scratched, and the St Clement passed the first stage. In the second tie the two local teams, St Clement and Dunmore, were drawn against each other, and Saturday was the day appointed for the contest. After a keen struggle the St Clement were victorious by three goals to nothing. Of course St Clement had the advantage being the older

and more experienced team, but the Dunmore on this occasion were represented by the best players from their own and other clubs in the district".

St. Clement's received a 'bye' in round three and landed a plum tie in the fourth round against Ayrshire side Beith. For reasons unknown, however, the Dundee side scratched from the Scottish Cup despite being one of the last eighteen teams remaining in the competition from an original entry of 116.

By this time a number of Association clubs were operating in and around Dundee and, during the remainder of season 1877/78, St. Clement's played out fixtures against a number of local teams, including East End and Strathmore; the formation of which will be portrayed in the following chapter.

Play was by no means confined to the local area, however, and in an attempt to improve the standard of play some testing fixtures were arranged against clubs of a higher calibre, including the much respected Glasgow Caledonian.

The game of Association football and the reputation of the St. Clement's club had also spread the short distance north-east to the fishing town of Arbroath during the 1877/78 season, which prompted budding players from the town's two rugby clubs to try their hand at the Association game. St Clement's were eventually persuaded to visit Arbroath in order to demonstrate how the game should be played and, on Saturday 16th March 1878, the very first Association football match to be played in Arbroath was contested between a scratch Arbroath side and St. Clement's on the town's Low Common. The event attracted much interest from the local population and was hailed as a huge success, as is evident from the report which appeared in the following Monday's Evening Telegraph:

"Some time ago a number of the players of the Arbroath Rovers and Arbroath Rugby Clubs began to play the game according to Association rules, and in order that the Association style may be

properly introduced they asked the St Clement some time ago to come down on a Saturday afternoon to do so. The match was played on the Low Common, and a very large number of spectators were present, who behaved admirably throughout. One feature very much admired by the Dundee players was the impartiality with which the onlookers hailed a good piece of play – Dundee coming in for their share of applause as well as the local team. They were also highly amused by the "heading" propensities of some of the players. The ground is not very well adapted for smart passing and dribbling, and some splendid opportunities were lost by both sides from the inequalities of the ground. In spite of this some very fast play was shown, and the Arbroath team contributed their share. During the first period Dundee scored four goals, and had pretty much their own way, but in the next Arbroath showed great improvement, and no more goals were taken. The ball was more than once carried into the territory of the St Clement, none of the shots taking effect, however. At the conclusion of the match the game was continued for about half-an-hour longer by mutual agreement, Arbroath apparently having much appreciated the friendly contest. The Arbroath would make a splendid Association team with some practice."

Shortly after this match was played, Arbroath Football Club was founded; the same famous old club that survives to this day!

Despite playing several challenge matches over the course of the following season, including a scheduled trip to Edinburgh to face Heart of Midlothian and home meetings with Dunbartonshire side Lenzie and the newly-founded Arbroath, it would appear that interest in the game from certain quarters within the club was starting to wane.

Despite being scheduled to play Arbroath for a second time in the 1878/79 Scottish Cup, the Dundee side decided to scratch from the competition for reasons unknown.

Little or no information regarding St. Clement's can be found following the club's decision to withdraw from that season's national tournament.

Although the team's name was entered into the hat for the Scottish Cup draw over the course of the following three seasons, they scratched from the competition on each occasion without even kicking a ball.

Despite having been founded amidst much enthusiasm just five years earlier, St. Clement's Football Club had disappeared completely from the sports columns of the local newspapers before the end of the 1881/82 season.

However, during their short existence, St Clement's had ignited a passion within the sports fraternity of Dundee for Association football, and it was this passion that led to the formation of several Association clubs in Dundee over the following years.

A footballer from the Victorian age dressed in typical nineteenth century outfit.

2

The Formation of East End

Following the foundation of the area's first Association football club, St. Clement's, several other football clubs were established in and around Dundee in a relatively short period of time; the first of these being the short-lived Dunmore, who were only briefly in existence from 1876 until 1878.

In 1877, two more Dundee football clubs joined the fold; namely Strathmore and East End. Both of these teams were destined to become well established in Dundee football circles, but arguably it was Strathmore who led the way as the most influential club during those early years.

The first match played by Strathmore Football Club, who played in black and white hoped jerseys, took place at Magdalen Green on Saturday 10th March 1877 against the aforementioned Dunmore, where the new club were no match for their more experienced opponents and went down by five goals without reply.

Four weeks later, the same two clubs faced each other at the same venue and, although Strathmore appeared to be an improved side, they still lost heavily, this time by four-goals-to-one.

Gradually, however, matters improved both on and off the field of play, with Strathmore's financial situation boosted considerably by donations from the club's patron, the Earl of Strathmore. The club had also started to attract more budding players than could be accommodated within one team and, by the end of the 1878/79 season, they found it necessary to operate a second eleven.

East End Football Club, who played in light blue and white stripes, were founded at around the same time as Strathmore. In fact, it is unclear which of the two sides was formed first!

East End initially played their home matches on Magdalen Green, along with Dundee's other Association football clubs at that time. What is rather intriguing, however, is why a club based at Magdalen Green, situated almost a mile to the west of the present-day Dundee city centre, should adopt the name East End? It is entirely possible that the club's founders hailed from the eastern end of Dundee, but if that was the case why did East End not set up home in that vicinity, perhaps at Baxter Park, which had already been used for Association matches by the time East End were founded? There is one possible explanation. At the time of the club's formation, there were two football pitches on Magdalen Green, one at the west end and one at the east end. Was East End Football Club so named because their home matches were played at the east end of Magdalen Green? We may never know!

The first match that can be traced involving East End Football Club took place on the afternoon of Saturday 31st March 1877, when a one-all draw was fought out with local side Dunmore on Magdalen Green. As the months progressed, East End grew in confidence, and eventually reckoned they were good enough to compete with Dundee's top side at the time, St Clement's. A match was duly arranged between the two clubs, to be played on Magdalen Green on the afternoon of Saturday 17th November 1877.

A large crowd turned out to witness the event, who were treated to some skilful play by the more fancied St Clement's side who, not surprisingly, won a rather one-sided match by four goals without reply. Despite the heavy defeat, however, East End could take some comfort from the fact that they had, on more than one occasion, given the best football club in Dundee a few uncomfortable moments.

Reporting on the match, the Dundee Courier was of the opinion that during the first half the East End had played *"in a plucky manner, and kept the play in the west end of the ground for a short time"*. In summing up, the same newspaper concluded: *"although they pressed their adversaries rather hard at times, they were unable to score"*.

Both East End and Strathmore continued to test their skills in challenge matches against other local sides whenever the opportunity arose; not only against the other Dundee clubs, but frequently both home and away against budding young teams from the surrounding towns and villages, including Arbroath, Forfar, Coupar Angus and Broughty Ferry.

However, there were still insufficient Association clubs in and around Dundee to fill a fixture list at that time, and on occasion local rugby teams were persuaded to temporarily switch codes in order to fill a blank Saturday. One such club was Tayside Rugby Club, who were easily beaten by East End on Magdalen Green in February 1878. *"It may be mentioned that the Tayside had always played Rugby before, and were consequently at a disadvantage"*, observed the local press.

Just a few weeks later, a 'return' match was played out between the same two clubs on Magdalen Green, in which East End once again emerged victorious, although Tayside had been, by all accounts, a much improved side. *"The game was very good one throughout, and was witnessed a large concourse of spectators"*, commented the Dundee Courier, who added that some additional excitement was enjoyed by the crowd when the football was accidentally kicked into the adjacent River Tay.

With there being no spare football available, one of the Tayside players jumped in to the freezing water in an attempt to retrieve the ball, and swam after it for several hundred yards, but eventually had to give up when it became evident that he was fighting a losing battle against the currents.

A boat was then launched to retrieve the ball, and the match was eventually resumed after a considerable delay!

These matches between East End Association Football Club and Tayside Rugby Club may have seemed of little significance at the time, but it later transpired that they had been, in actual fact, of significant importance in the history of Association football in Dundee, and in the formation of a certain football club some fifteen years later.

All will become clear in the following chapter!

3

Our Boys Enter the Fray

Tayside Rugby Club, who are believed to have been founded in 1872, established themselves as a respected side in Dundee and the surrounding area during the 1870's, regularly playing matches against sides of similar standing from the likes of Perth, Arbroath, Cupar and St. Andrews. Indeed, the club was even mentioned as far away as London in March 1874, when the 'Sporting Gazette' gave a brief mention of their encounter with Broughty Ferry side Artisan on Magdalen Green!

With the rise in popularity of the Association game in Dundee during the late 1870's, however, the Tayside players decided to try their hand at the new code, and their first encounter with the round ball, against East End in February 1878, was described in the previous chapter.

On Thursday 22nd August 1878, Tayside Rugby club held its annual meeting, when Team Captain James Dron, Club Secretary Tom Greig, Treasurer William Buchanan and Committee Members Arthur and Westwater discussed, along with the other club members present, the possibility of disbanding their Rugby club and forming an Association football club, following the success of their two matches against East End earlier that year.

These discussions must have been met with approval by all concerned, because just over a week later, on Monday 2nd September 1878, a report appeared in the local press stating that, at a meeting of newly-founded Our Boys Football Club, the same club officials who had attended the annual meeting of Tayside rugby club had now been appointed to exactly the same positions with Our Boys F.C. From that day onwards, Tayside Rugby Club ceased to exist.

Many years later, when speaking at a club function in the Thistle Hall, the then Honorary President of Our Boys, Bailie Hunter, recalled the formation of the club during an address to the local dignitaries and club officials present:

"Our Boys originated in the Tayside, the members of which played under Rugby rules. When the Association game began to take such a hold on Scotch football players the Tayside, along with many other clubs, abandoned their old mode of play and adopted the new code. They were thorough radicals, for not only did they change their mode of play, but they also changed their name".

Dundee now had another Association football team, and the new club, who played in scarlet and black striped jerseys, wasted no time in gaining membership of the Scottish Football Association. As members of the Association, the Dundee Our Boys name was also entered into the forthcoming Scottish Cup competition for season 1878/79.

At a meeting of the S.F.A., on Tuesday 10th September 1878, Our Boys were drawn to face Arbroath; another young club whose foundation was described in a previous chapter. Although Our Boys had been drawn at home, they elected to play the match at Woodville, about two miles inland from Arbroath, on Saturday 28th September 1878.

As far as can be ascertained, this was the first match played by the club under the Our Boys name and, being a Scottish Cup tie, the game was given considerable coverage in the local press.

The Dundee Evening Telegraph, who commented that the park at Woodville *"was admirably suited for the game, being almost dead level"*, also observed that one of the Our Boys players had been rendered *"hors de combat"* following an incident at the beginning of the match, and the Dundee team were consequently a weaker side. Arbroath, by all accounts, were the stronger of the two teams throughout the game and, during the first half, *"pressed their opponents hard"*.

Leading by a single goal at half-time, Arbroath continued to dominate during the second half, and scored a further two goals to win the match 3-0. In fact, the winning margin could well have been greater had a fourth goal not been disallowed when the ball was adjudged to have rebounded off one of the spectators, who was standing close to the touch-line, before being placed between the posts.

Despite this initial defeat, Our Boys were not disheartened, and quickly arranged two challenge matches against the formidable Heart of Midlothian; the first of which was to be played on The Meadows in Edinburgh on Thursday 24th October 1878. As one would expect, Our Boys were no match for a side already well established in Scottish Football, and unsurprisingly went down 5-0.

Exactly a week later, a large crowd turned out at Magdalen Green for the return match, where unfortunately for the home side an identical score-line was recorded. In summing up their report on the encounter, the Dundee Courier commented:

"the whole of the strangers exhibited fine play and good tactics; while one or two of the Dundee men, and especially those on the left wing, strove skilfully to retrieve their lost laurels".

On Saturday 30th November 1878, Our Boys recorded what is thought to have been their first-ever victory, when East End were defeated by a single goal on Magdalen Green. With the ground in very poor condition, good football was rendered impossible; but, despite the slippery conditions, Our Boys by all accounts dominated the match and created several goal-scoring opportunities, only to be denied by the brilliance of the East End 'keeper. Ironically, it was a mistake by the same custodian that allowed Our Boys to register the only goal of the game, deep into the second half.

Over the weeks and months that followed, Our Boys played regularly on the Magdalen Green, where they faced Strathmore on at least two occasions.

The club also ventured further afield as the season progressed, and on 8th February 1879 defeated Coupar Angus on their own soil by two-goals-to-one.

In the return match against Coupar Angus on Saturday 8th March 1879, which interestingly was played at BaxterPark, Our Boys again emerged victorious by four goals without reply in a rather one-sided game, during which, according to the match report which appeared in the Dundee Courier, the team had displayed some *"splendid passing"*.

Later that same month, Our Boys and East End faced each other for a second time on a wind-swept Magdalen Green, and any hopes that East End might have had of revenge following their defeat earlier in the season were blown away by a confident display from Our Boys, who, for their second game in succession, scored four goals without reply.

Our Boys reputation had been growing steadily over the course of their inaugural season and, as well as attracting large crowds to their matches, they were also attracting the attentions of several budding footballers who wanted to become involved in playing the game. As a result, Our Boys introduced a second eleven towards the end of the 1878/79 season

On Saturday 5th April, Our Boys' second string played their first match, against the second eleven of Strathmore, who had also been attracting more playing members. The result was yet another emphatic victory for 'The Boys', and the future of the club looked very rosy indeed!

Our Boys rounded off a very successful first season on Saturday 3rd May with a match on Magdalen Green against the 50th Queen's Own Regiment, who were stationed in the local barracks at the time. Incredibly, if the newspaper reports of this match are to be believed, almost 5,000 spectators witnessed the game, but this seems rather unlikely!

Yet another four-nil victory was the result, although it has to be said that the soldiers were *"not very well up to the Association rules"* according to press reports.

It was, nevertheless, another fine performance, and it was now clear that Our Boys had, after just one season, firmly established themselves as one of Dundee's top Association football clubs.

Victorian Football Action
(from a nineteenth-century etching)

4

Early Days

At the beginning of the 1879/80 football season, the four established Association football clubs in Dundee; namely St Clement's, Strathmore, East End and Our Boys; were joined by the newly-founded Dundee Harp and Dundee Hibernian. As the names might suggest, both of these clubs had their roots set firmly in the large Irish immigrant population that had arrived in Dundee during the mid-nineteenth century to take advantage of the employment opportunities that existed in the textile, building, shipping and railway construction industries.

Harp, who were founded at a meeting of the St Patrick's Young Men's Society on the evening of Monday 29th July 1879, were also destined to become firmly established in the higher echelons of local football over the coming years. They played their first match on the evening of Thursday 4th August on Magdalen Green against Our Boys, who won by four goals to nothing. Dundee Hibernian's inaugural match was played the following month, when they faced Harp at the same venue.

Another Dundee side founded at this time was the intriguingly named Perseverance F.C., who were also to become established as a formidable local side over the following decade. With these new clubs still in their infancy, and with St Clement's now in demise, the three teams who now dominated the local football scene were Strathmore, East End and Our Boys. The newspapers of the time also give mention to a Dundee Football Club founded in or around

1879, but further details of this short-lived club seem to have been lost in the mists of time.

The first local competitive match of season 1879/80 was played on 20th September, when Our Boys faced Arbroath in the Scottish Cup for the second year in a row. This time, the game was played *"in a field near Elliot"*, on the south-western approach to the seaside town where, in front of a large crowd, the home side repeated their feat of the previous season by knocking Our Boys out of the competition, this time by five-goals-to-one.

Strathmore, who were given a 'bye' in the first round, were awarded a 'walk-over' against local rivals St Clement's in round two, before losing 6-1 to Our Boys' conquerors Arbroath at the third stage of the competition.

During Our Boys' rapid rise to become one of the top three clubs in Dundee during their existence of just over a year, the other top clubs, East End and Strathmore, had also grown steadily in stature. All three were ambitious clubs, and it was inevitable that they would eventually have to procure their own home grounds rather than share the public football parks on the Magdalen Green.

This need for football grounds to call their own became more pressing when, in November 1879, a skating rink was built over one of the Magdalen Green pitches, much to the annoyance of the increasing number of local football 'enthusiasts' who regularly used the facilities. With BaxterPark by this time *"reserved by those in authority for inter-town and county matches"*, it looked very much like the remaining pitches on Magdalen Green were going to be extremely cramped places on Saturdays!

The first club to relocate was Our Boys, who secured a short-term rental of land adjacent to Lawton Farm, immediately to the north of Dundee Law, which they named LawtonPark.

They remained at LawtonPark for most of the 1879/80 campaign, during which they played host to a number of clubs from Dundee and the surrounding area.

As far as can be ascertained, the first match to take place at Lawton Park was against Coupar Angus side Vale of Strathmore, who were beaten 1-0 in October 1879. The following month, Our Boys played host to the aforementioned but apparently short lived early incarnation of a team by the name of Dundee F.C.

LawtonPark had its limits, however, and from information gleaned from match reports at this time it appears that the ground had a bad slope running the length of the park from west to east. It was also in a rather exposed and windswept position, making it vulnerable to wintry weather.

It must also be remembered that LawtonPark would not have been a traditional football ground, but merely a roughly adapted field surrounded by a hedge. In all probability, this field would only have been available to rent from the farmer for a limited time during the period from late autumn until it was required for grazing once again in the following spring!

It is probably for these reasons that, when Our Boys attracted teams of a higher calibre to Dundee, they opted to use BaxterPark. This was the preferred venue for the visit of Lenzie on 29th November 1879, when Our Boys recorded a rather impressive 2-1 victory *"in presence of a large number who unfortunately often came inside the flagposts"*.

Baxter Park had probably been used as the venue for the visit of Hearts a few weeks earlier, when 'The Boys' went down by six-goals-to-three, but match reports do not state where this game was actually played.

During the early days of football in Dundee, only very severe weather would force the cancellation of a match. Several reports of the time speak of games going ahead on

The TayRailwayBridge following the disaster on 27th December 1879, as seen from Magdalen Green.

frost-bound pitches and of matches taking place on football grounds covered in several inches of snow. Tales of games being played in blizzard conditions with gale-force winds interfering with good play were not uncommon.

The weather conditions on Saturday 27th December 1879 must have been extreme, therefore, for there to be no matches played at all in Dundee. In fact, very few matches were played in Scotland that day; and of those that did go ahead, several were abandoned at half-time due to gale-force winds and torrential rain.

One game that was played to a finish, however, was the unofficial British Championship decider between Scottish Cup holders Vale of Leven and English F.A. Cup holders Old Etonians at Hampden Park where, according to the Glasgow Herald: *"the rain came down in buckets, aggravated by the impulsion of a fitful gale of wind, in which hats and umbrellas suffered alarmingly"*. Only a handful of spectators held out until the conclusion of the match, which finished 5-2 in favour of the Scottish team.

The storm raged on unabated throughout the following day, eventually reaching near-hurricane force in Dundee. Early that evening, just as the Burntisland to Dundee train was crossing the Tay Railway Bridge, the bridge succumbed to the severe buffeting from the gale and collapsed into the river, taking with it the engine, the coaches, and the lives of 100 poor souls.

For several years following the disaster, football matches on the Magdalen Green were played against a backdrop of what remained of that ill-fated first Tay Bridge.

Our Boys played out the remainder of season 1879/80 in rampant form, and recorded some convincing victories, including an 8-1 thumping of Strathmore and a 4-0 success against Coupar Angus. There could be no doubt that Our

Boys had now become established as Dundee's top team and, at their annual meeting on Thursday 29th April 1880, the reports submitted by the Secretary and Treasurer showed the club to be *"in a flourishing condition"*.

During the season just finished, Our Boys had played twelve matches, of which nine had been won, two lost, and one drawn. The record of the second eleven was equally impressive, with seven victories and two draws recorded from nine matches played.

However, Our Boys were now without a home ground, as their agreement to rent the field at Lawton Farm had now expired. In order to raise funds to secure a new park, the club organized a concert in the Thistle Hall, where *"a large and well selected programme of songs was provided"*, including renditions from a Mr. T. Philips, whose *"songs were full of humour and witticisms; the expressive style in which he rendered them never failed to amuse"*. The event proved to be highly successful, and the club raised sufficient funds to allow them to enter into negotiations for the rental of a suitable home venue for the forthcoming season.

East End, on the other hand, had not exactly set the heather alight during the 1879/80 season. Matches played by the club were few and far between, possibly due to the high demand for the greatly reduced football facilities at Magdalen Green, on which an increasing number of clubs were now competing for space on which to play. Of the East End games that did go ahead on Magdalen Green, they appear to have been seen as of little significance by the local press and not worthy of reporting.

During the latter part of the season, however, two matches played by East End did find their way into the sports columns; a meeting with Our Boys at Lawton Park in late January 1880, where a 2-0 win for the home side was the outcome; and a trip up the coast to Arbroath a week later, which also ended in defeat, this time by three-goals-to-nil.

As the end of the season loomed, it looked very much like East End, on the field of play at least, were about to be eclipsed by some of the other local teams.

Financially, however, the club was still *"in a very prosperous state"*, according to Treasurer and Secretary William McLean, who added that the club had *"a good balance at the credit of their account"*.

The number of Association football clubs based in the towns and villages situated within a few miles of Dundee was by this time increasing rapidly. Teams from places such as Montrose and Brechin had now become established, and joined the existing provincial clubs in Broughty Ferry, Coupar Angus and Arbroath on the list of possible opponents for the Dundee sides. Even village clubs such as Alyth were now starting to make their presence known.

For the 1880/81 Scottish Cup competition, Dundee clubs Our Boys, Strathmore and St. Clement's were entered into the hat for the first round, alongside fellow Forfarshire and Perthshire clubs Arbroath, Dunkeld, Rob Roy (Callander), Vale of Teith (Doune), and Coupar Angus.

Our Boys exited the competition at the first hurdle for the third season in succession after losing to Rob Roy in Callander by two-goals-to-one. As for the other Dundee clubs, Strathmore went down 4-1 at Coupar Angus, whilst St Clement's scratched from the tournament for the third season in a row.

Shortly after their Scottish Cup exit, Our Boys announced that they had secured the use of a new park situated directly to the south of East Clepington farm house, which they appropriately named ClepingtonPark.

As was the case with their previous ground, LawtonPark, this new ground would have simply been a field enclosed within a boundary of trees or a hedge. In later years, however, the south side of this field, referred to locally as 'CooPark', was to be developed into a fully-enclosed football ground, also called ClepingtonPark, before eventually being transformed into the present-day TannadicePark, home of Dundee United!

East End, however, were still playing their home games on Magdalen Green. Performances on the field of play were improving, though, and the club was now managing to operate a second eleven despite the limited recreation facilities Magdalen Green had to offer.

On Saturday 23rd October 1880, Our Boys and East End faced each other at ClepingtonPark for the first time, and the greatly-improved form of the visitors was apparent when they established a single-goal half-time lead. Despite a spirited performance from East End during the second period, however, the home side scored twice to win the match 2-1.

Encouraged by this display against the more fancied Our Boys, a confident East End shared the spoils with Strathmore on Magdalen Green just a week later, in a game they really should have won after hitting the post twice during the second half. Undeterred, they travelled east to Broughty Ferry on Saturday 6th November, where they finally got back to winning ways with an impressive 4-0 victory over the home side.

Towards the end of November, East End once again had the opportunity to test their skills against one of the more fancied teams, in a home fixture against Arbroath. In anticipation of a larger than usual crowd, the club was granted permission to use Baxter Park for the occasion, where a closely fought encounter, described as *"very pleasant throughout"*, ended in a 1-1 draw. East End's reputation was once again on the rise.

Meanwhile, at ClepingtonPark, Our Boys were sweeping all before them and, in front of a large crowd on Saturday 13th November, they demolished Strathmore by nine-goals-without reply. This heavy defeat for Strathmore, along with East End's recent resurgence, fuelled general opinion in Dundee football circles over the following weeks that it was East End and Our Boys who were now the two best teams in the local area.

That theory was backed up when, reporting on East End's second visit of the season to play Our Boys at ClepingtonPark on Christmas Day 1880, the Dundee Courier made the following observation:

"The weather was very stormy and cold, but, notwithstanding, the turnout of spectators was good, which shows the interest that is taken in football in this district, now that the two principal clubs north of the Tay belong to Dundee".

East End certainly lived up to their new reputation, and by all accounts gave Our Boys a stiff test. In the end, however, they were unfortunate to lose a closely fought battle by a single goal in conditions that were far from perfect.

It was inevitable that eventually Our Boys would be brought down to earth, and this happened on a snow-covered ClepingtonPark on 19th February 1881 when Arbroath, who had remained unbeaten all season, paid a visit. Despite the best efforts of the home side, Arbroath scored four times without reply to inflict a humiliating defeat in front of several hundred home supporters.

However, it didn't take Our Boys long to gain revenge and, on Saturday 2nd April 1881, a ding-dong battle at Gayfield ended in favour of Our Boys by the odd-goal-in-five to inflict a first defeat of the season on Arbroath, whose defence was said to have been *"pretty well fagged out"* when the final whistle blew!

Two weeks later, Our Boys confirmed their position as Dundee's top team when they thumped Strathmore 5-1 on the Magdalen Green, before the season was rounded off at the same venue on 30th April with yet another meeting with East End, when unfortunately tempers became rather frayed.

Despite a strong gale-force wind blowing into their faces, Our Boys scored the opening goal during the first half, and managed to hold on to their lead until half-time.

Twenty minutes into the second period, the Boys thought they had doubled their advantage, but East End claimed that one of their players had been fouled in the build up to the goal.

An argument then ensued and several East End players marched off the field and refused to continue. And there ended the 1880/81 football season as far as Our Boys and East End were concerned!

5

An Intense Rivalry Starts to Build

East End finally managed to procure a ground to call their own not long after the commencement of the 1881/82 season when they agreed terms with the landowner of a field at the top of Provost Road, a few hundred yards to the north of the present-day DensPark, the current home of Dundee Football Club. The new ground was christened Havercroft Park, and must have been at least partially enclosed, probably by a hedge, because the club was now able to charge for entry to their matches, with patrons charged 3d for the privilege (1½ pence in today's money). Ladies were admitted free of charge.

However, as far as home grounds were concerned, both East End and Our Boys were now envious of Strathmore. During the summer of 1881, the 'Strathie' had appointed a committee with the sole purpose of seeking out a suitable home ground near to the centre of Dundee and, after much negotiating, they secured the exclusive use of Rollo's Pier, an established sports ground located immediately to the south of Magdalen Yard Road (on the portion of that road now known as Roseangle), close to its junction with Perth Road. The site of the ground is today occupied by the Seabraes Court student accommodation associated with DundeeUniversity.

Also known as the Roseangle Recreation Grounds, Rollo's Pier, as the name might suggest, had once formed part of a small harbour area on the north shore of the Firth of Tay. When the Dundee to Perth Railway was opened in the late 1840's, the route of the line took it along a newly-built causeway, about a hundred yards to the south of the pier, which effectively cut the harbour area off from the firth.

An artist's impression of Rollo's Pier, the home ground of Strathmore from 1881 until 1890. This depiction of Rollo's Pier is believed to be accurate, apart from the position and size of the grandstand, of which very little detail is actually known.

It is also quite possible that the structure was roofless, as was the case with many grandstands at this time.

What had once been the harbour was then filled in and, being a relatively flat piece of land, it had been deemed suitable for recreational purposes.

For several years before Strathmore took up residence, the land at Rollo's Pier, on which a grandstand had been erected, had been used for sports meetings as well as for dancing during the summer months.

The ground was accessed via a steep embankment on the south side of Magdalen Yard Road, which also served as a vantage point for spectators. Tunneling under the lower part of the embankment were several arches, which were used as changing facilities and for storage purposes. These arches had, in all probability, once been used as warehouses; a throwback to the days when goods had been shipped from the pier.

The playing surface, which had been previously described as *"being laid out in the form of a lawn"*, was surrounded by an oval running track of around 220 yards (approximately 200 metres) in length.

Once the use of Rollo's Pier had been secured, Strathmore wasted little time in developing and enclosing the ground. When the renovations were complete, the club's efforts came in for much praise from the local press, with the Dundee Courier observing:

"The Strathmore Football Club sometime ago appointed a Committee to look out for ground about the centre of the town, and they accordingly entered into negotiations with the proprietors of Rollo's Pier, and are now glad to be able to state that these negotiations have resulted in the Strathmore having obtained the use of the Pier; and during the past two or three months workmen have been busily engaged at the Pier in filling up and levelling the ground and enclosing it. One of the arches underneath Magdalen Yard Road has been turned into a spacious dressing room, which has been fitted up in a very comfortable and substantial manner".

"The grand stand has also been thoroughly repaired, new flooring and railing having been inserted, and, altogether, the pier, with its excellent appointments and central locality, may now be safely considered one the finest and most desirable private grounds belonging to any football club in the north-east of Scotland. All this has necessarily been done at a large expense, and we trust that the public will turn out at the matches in numbers sufficient to recoup the Strathmore for its outlay."

Although the attendances at both East End and Our Boys matches were increasing steadily, there could be no doubt that Strathmore, being located almost in the centre of Dundee, would now be able to attract the biggest crowds as they were based closer to the more populated parts of the Burgh.

The first match to be played Rollo's Pier was a Scottish Cup third round tie between Strathmore and Our Boys on 29th October 1881, which went ahead *"in presence of a large number of spectators"*. Strathmore may have procured the best football ground in Dundee, but Our Boys still held the upper hand on the field of play, and duly romped home by four-goals-to one.

Our Boys' cup run during season 1881/82 was their best to date, and their convincing victory at Rollo's Pier saw the club reach the last twenty-two in the national competition. After having finally managed to overcome Arbroath in the first round (at the third time of asking!), they knocked local rivals Dundee Harp out of the tournament in a second round replay by five-goals-to-three at Clepington Park following a one-all draw.

Their reward for beating Strathmore in the third round was a trip to Kilmarnock on 19th November, where unsurprisingly the home side won convincingly by nine-goals-to-two.

Our Boys' reputation was now such that the club was able to attract bigger clubs for challenge matches and, on 3rd January 1882, Glasgow Rangers visited ClepingtonPark.

In what is believed to have been the first time the Glasgow side had visited Dundee, an entertaining encounter ended all-square at a goal-apiece.

This match was closely followed by a visit from another Glasgow club, South Western, who won 6-0 in a match described as *"very agreeable and well-contested throughout"*.

An intense rivalry was starting to build at this time between the more established Dundee clubs and their growing number of followers. Matches between the local clubs were now keenly fought affairs, and there was certainly no love lost between the players or the supporters in these 'derby' games.

One such meeting between rival Dundee clubs took place at HavercroftPark in January 1882, when East End played host to Our Boys. On a bitterly cold afternoon, with snow covering the ground, the home side quickly raced to a two goal lead, aided in no small way by a strong wind at their backs. Our Boys refused to lie down, however, and managed to pull a goal back before half-time. By the time the second half got under way, the wind had increased to gale-force, and the visitors took full advantage of the conditions to turn the game around and lead by three-goals-to-two.

It was at this point that the match degenerated into a farce.

"Now the fun grew fast and furious", reported the Dundee Evening Telegraph, who continued: *"Charging seemed to be the order of the day, consequently some coarse play was shown, which was immensely enjoyed by the onlookers. As each man came to grief a burst of laughter and cheering followed"*.

Despite playing into the wind, East End eventually managed to force the ball home to equalise matters then, just moments later, they appeared to have regained the lead, much to the delight of the home supporters. Our Boys, however, disputed the goal, claiming that a hand had been used.

Public Notices

FOOTBALL MATCH
ARBROATH v. EAST END

Saturday 5th Nov., at Havercroft Park (Top of Provost Road).

Kick off at 3:30 prompt.

Admission 3d. Ladies Free.

GRAND FOOTBALL MATCH

OUR BOYS v. STRATHMORE on SATURDAY

First, 5th November, in PARK at CLEPINGTON FARM. Kick Off at 3 o'clock prompt. Admission 3d., Ladies Free.

With clubs now able to charge for admission after having obtained their own "private" grounds, advertisements for matches started to appear regularly in the local press.

A fierce squabble then ensued, during which several East End players left the field. The goal was then disallowed, and for a while it appeared that the game was to be abandoned. Once order had been restored, however, the missing East End players were persuaded to return to the field, and the match was played to a finish without further incident.

As the end of the 1881/82 season approached, Our Boys decided that the time was right to find a permanent home for the club after having spent two seasons renting the field at Clepington Farm. As the game of Association football had grown in popularity over the preceding years, the clubs who played on rented farm land were now finding that the situation was far from ideal. With rented fields only being available during the winter months, teams were now finding it increasingly difficult to accommodate their growing fixture lists, and this was a problem that could only be overcome if these clubs had grounds they could truly call their own.

This dilemma was highlighted towards the end of season 1881/82, when Our Boys had to borrow Rollo's Pier from Strathmore in order to play their 'home' friendlies against west of Scotland sides Lenzie and Abercorn. With large crowds turning out for the games, both of which were played in warm and dry conditions ideal for football, the benefits of having the luxury of a private home ground at this time of the year was becoming increasingly apparent.

Before the commencement of season 1882/83, Our Boys overcame the problem by leasing land adjacent to West Craigie Farm, on the north side of Arbroath Road and immediately to the west of BaxterPark. The club wasted no time in transforming the piece of land into a football ground, to which they gave the name WestCraigiePark. This was to be Our Boys' home ground for over a decade. It is also thought that the club changed its colours at around this time, from scarlet and black stripes to dark blue.

With Clepington Park now vacant, East End decided to take advantage of the situation, and moved their headquarters the relatively short distance of just a few hundred yards south-east from HavercroftPark after having agreed terms with the land owner.

Although ClepingtonPark was, just like HavercroftPark, essentially rented farm land, it would appear from all accounts that it was an improvement on the club's previous home ground, as is evident from the following article which appeared in the Dundee Courier on Monday 24th July 1882:

"We understand that the East End Football Club has secured for the ensuing season from Mr. Cooper, Clepington, the park situated immediately in front of his house. As the Club has already some important fixtures on their card, and are presently negotiating with some first-rate clubs for the purpose of playing matches with them, a brilliant season may be confidently anticipated".

Just weeks later, on Saturday 9th September 1882, East End played their first-ever Scottish Cup tie, against Arbroath at Gayfield. In an incredible match, the Dundee side raced to a three-nil half-time lead, and it looked like they were about to add a fourth goal during the second half, but one of the Arbroath defenders punched the ball clear just as it was about to cross the line.

Despite protests from the East End players that a goal should be awarded, the referee decided that a free-kick should be given instead (there was no such thing as a penalty kick until 1891!), which subsequently came to nothing.

Sensing that their opponents had been disheartened at the referee's decision, Arbroath seized the opportunity to take advantage of East End's despondency and, roared on by the home crowd, scored a remarkable four times in a matter of just a few minutes to turn the match around and snatch victory from the jaws of defeat.

Meanwhile, on the same day that East End played in their first-ever Scottish Cup tie, Our Boys played the first match of any significance at their new West Craigie home when they hosted Dundee Hibernians in the first round of the national competition.

Our Boys' opening match at their new ground turned out to be a rather one-sided game and ended favour of the home side by five-goals-to-one. It was, nevertheless, described by the press as *"a very pleasant and enjoyable one throughout"*.

In the second round of the competition, Our Boys were drawn to face Balgay, a new club who hailed from the west end of Dundee, who were successfully overcome by five-goals-to-two. The third round of the competition, played on 28th October 1882, saw Our Boys make the journey west to the Perthshire village of Doune, a few miles to the north-west of Stirling, to play local side Vale of Teith, where the Dundee side exited the Scottish Cup following a 6-4 defeat.

This reverse seemed to knock the wind out of Our Boys' sails for a while, as they slumped to surprise defeats from local rivals West End and Strathmore over the following weeks, with Strathmore's win at West Craigie recorded as being their first-ever victory against Our Boys!

However, the club did regain some respect when they challenged Vale of Teith, their conquerors in the Scottish Cup, to a challenge match at West Craigie at the end of November, where a closely contested and very entertaining game ended 2-1 in favour of the home side. *"The play all through was splendid"*, commented the Dundee Courier, who concluded: *"the opinion freely expressed was that this was one of the best games ever played in Dundee"*.

It was East End, however, who surprisingly managed to attract a higher calibre of opposition to Dundee for friendly encounters as the season progressed.

It had been anticipated that, after the club had taken up residence in Clepington Park, they would be able to play host to more respectable visiting sides than they had played at Havercroft Park, and their New Year programme of challenge matches did not disappoint.

In the first of these matches, against Glasgow side Whitefield on Saturday 30th December 1882, East End recorded a comfortable 3-0 victory to instill confidence within the players for the New Year's Day visit of Third Lanark, a club who had, during their short history, already managed to reach the final of the Scottish Cup on two occasions.

Unfortunately, conditions were far from perfect for the match. A thick mist lay on Clepington Park and, with the underfoot conditions described as soft, there was never going to be a lot of good football on display, although East End started the game well and shocked their more fancied opponents with an early goal. The Glasgow side soon cancelled out this advantage, however, and by half-time had established a 3-1 lead. The 'Thirds' continued to dominate during the second period, and the game eventually ended in defeat for East End by five-goals-to-two.

There was to be further disappointment on the following afternoon when the series of New Year challenge matches was wound up with defeat at the hands of Dunfermline. For the record, this team was not Dunfermline Athletic, who were not founded until 1885!

Our Boys' season started to pick up during the early months of 1883, with local club Perseverance beaten 7-1 at West Craigie closely followed by sweet revenge against Strathmore at Rollo's Pier by an incredible score of eight goals without reply. This defeat proved to be too much to take for one Strathmore supporter, however, who vented his feelings via the Dundee Courier's 'Letters to the Editor' column on Wednesday 28th February.

In a rant about Our Boys' apparent *"rough and tumble"* style, the correspondent, who simply signed his letter 'D.A.J.' claimed that there had been *"a wholesale tramping underfoot"* by the visiting team.

On one occasion, one of the Strathmore backs had been *"mounted 'cockerty huey' across the shoulders of some of the opposite side"*. The letter concluded: *"If our county is to rise to pre-eminence in the football world, such vagaries must be discouraged as much as possible, and as often as they are engaged in"*.

The intense rivalry that now existed between the supporters of the top Dundee teams came to the fore again just a couple of days later, when an Our Boys supporter, identifying himself as 'A.A.R.' used the same publication to hit back at the accusations.

"It is quite apparent that 'D. A. J.' is still smarting keenly from the defeat the 'light and speedy' received the hands of their opponents on Saturday at Rollo's Pier", he proclaimed; before adding that he thought it unwise to be expressing *"a lame excuse for their big defeat"* through the medium of the local press. *"I cannot imagine where 'D. A. J.' has gathered his wild and erroneous ideas of the match"*, he concluded.

However, the writer of the original letter found a friend in another correspondent calling himself 'True Game', who was quite clear that the rough conduct shown by Our Boys was done simply to gain some sort of revenge for their surprise defeat when the two teams had last met:

"Sir, – Having also been a spectator of the so called match at Rollo's Pier on Saturday afternoon last, I can fully corroborate all that is said regarding it by 'D.A.J.' Throughout, but more especially during the latter part of the game, the victors showed an utter disregard of the rules of football, and in the instance particularly referred to by your correspondent, the conduct exhibited deserved the severest condemnation of the large assemblage of spectators.

I may mention that during the match one of the 'Boys' made a savage rush against, or in technical parlance 'went for', an opponent, whose true and spirited play merited the warm encomiums passed upon it. He fortunately missed his mark, however, and measured his own length on the ground, the fall resulting, I heard, in the dislocation of one of his arms, and causing his retirement from the field. It is needless to say that the remark 'Served him right,' was far more common than any expression of compassion. A little later, if for the purpose of equalising the numerical strength of the teams, another 'Boy' overthrew a leading forward of the Strathmore, who was so viciously kicked that had also to be assisted off the ground. And this and all the rest for the sole reason apparently that the Strathmore were the victors on the former occasion".

And there the bickering concluded. At least until the next game!

Our Boys saw out the remainder of the season with several challenge matches against both local sides and teams from further afield, including a visit from Hamilton Academical at the beginning of April. Being the sole tenants of their home ground, they were now enjoying the fact that they could play at West Craigie whenever they liked.

East End, on the other hand, were still at the mercy of the landowner, and it would appear that they were unable to play home matches towards the end of the 1882/83 season, as no reports of matches played at Clepington Park appeared in the press. The club did, however, record a single-goal victory against Strathmore at Rollo's Pier at the beginning of April. It was now clear that, in order to compete with the best, East End would have to follow in the footsteps of Our Boys and secure a permanent home.

What the Association game really needed in Dundee and the surrounding area, however, was competitive matches rather than the series of challenge games that currently took up the majority of the football season.

6

The Forfarshire Football Association

As mentioned in the previous chapter, Association football clubs in Dundee and the local area were, by this time, becoming a little bored with the lack of competitive matches played during the season.

With over twenty well-established teams now playing in the geographical area stretching eastwards from Dundee as far as Montrose and north-west to Coupar Angus, twelve of which were considered good enough to compete in the Scottish Cup, feeling was high that the clubs concerned were crying out for a local cup competition to be inaugurated. The clubs concerned were also of the opinion that they would benefit greatly from being governed by a local Association.

With this in mind, in January 1883, all interested parties were called to a meeting in Dundee's Imperial Hotel, with a view to forming a Football Association to represent the local area. With Strathmore's William Robertson in the chair, a proposal was put forward that:

"an Association for the county be formed, with a challenge cup to be competed for annually by the various Clubs in the county".

The proposal was agreed to, and the Forfarshire Football Association was inaugurated with the aforementioned William Robertson of Strathmore elected as President; Our Boys' W.E. Buchanan as Vice-President; East End's Robert Smart as Treasurer and Mr. Scott from the Broughty Ferry club as Secretary. A Committee was also formed with representatives from the Strathmore, Our Boys, East End, Arbroath, Harp, West End, Perseverance and Balgay clubs.

It was also resolved at the same meeting that a cup be purchased for the princely sum of £30; the money to be raised *"by subscription among the various clubs and also from the proceeds of certain exhibition matches, to be afterwards arranged"*.

The first of the aforementioned fund-raising exhibition matches took place at West Craigie on 21st April 1883, where East End recorded a comfortable 3-1 victory over hosts Our Boys in front of *"a pretty fair amount of spectators"*. The gate money raised amounted to £10-15s (£10.75), which prompted the Dundee Advertiser to comment that, financially, *"a pretty good start has been made"*.

Other exhibition matches and fund-raising activities then followed, and funds to purchase the CountyCup were duly raised as planned. At the beginning of the following season, 1883/84, the draw for the first round of the new competition was made with no fewer than eighteen clubs participating:

Windmill (Dundee) v Dundee West End
Arbroath v Our Boys
Perseverance (Dundee) v Arbroath Strathmore
Montrose United v Seafield (Dundee)
Clydesdale (Dundee) v Strathtay (Dundee)
Dundee East End v Dundee Hibernians
Coupar Angus v Avondale (Lochee)
Dundee Strathmore v Balgay (Dundee)
Dundee Harp v Broughty Ferry

The trophy itself was described as a *"magnificent specimen of the silversmith's art"*, and was put on display in the window of Dundee High Street jeweller Harry Tulloch.

Describing the coveted prize, the Dundee Courier enthused:

"Standing about 20 inches in height, the cup is of elegant design, and is richly chased, while the beautifully embossed Scotch thistles give it national character".

"On one side is a representation of part of a football field, with two or three players in costume contending for the ball, and the goalkeeper between the posts, while on the other is the title of the Association".

With most of the local clubs now running at least two teams, the decision was made in September 1883 to form a Forfarshire Second Eleven Association, and to hold an annual Challenge Cup tournament to be competed for in the same manner as the main county competition. The Second Eleven Association was duly inaugurated on 4th October 1883, with Mr John Smith of Harp elected as Chairman; Arbroath's Harry Clark elected Vice-Chairman; Strathmore's Charlie Howe installed as Secretary, and Our Boys' James Ritchie appointed Treasurer.

Before the first-ever Forfarshire Cup tournament got under way, East End were successful in securing a new home ground, which they reported had been secured *"for a considerable term"* from local land owner Francis Batchelor. It was hoped that the new park was one on which the club would be able to play for the whole season, and not one which they could be forced out of whenever the land owner saw fit, as had happened at previous grounds.

East End's new park was located in the Stobsmuir area of Dundee, near MorganHospital (later MorganAcademy), just a few hundred yards to the north of Our Boys' West Craigie ground. The exact location of the new park was pinpointed in an article which appeared in the Dundee Advertiser on Saturday 1st September 1883:

"New Park for Football. – The East End Football Club have secured from Mr Batchelor, Craigie, for a considerable term, a park in Madeira Street, which runs between Pitkerro and Forfar Roads. The entrance to the park is at the back of the MorganHospital, immediately opposite Maryfield Bowling Green".

"The ground will be known by the name of MadeiraPark, and will be opened this day week (8th September) by the Strathmore in the first round of the Scottish Association Cup Tie".

Unfortunately, the opening of East End's MadeiraPark was not a happy occasion, with local rivals Strathmore progressing to round two of the national competition following a single-goal victory.

Exactly two weeks later, however, on 22nd September 1883, East End competed in their first-ever Forfarshire Cup tie, when they thumped Dundee Hibernians by eight goals to nothing at MadeiraPark. Indeed, by all accounts the score could have been much higher but for a great display of goalkeeping by the Hibs' 'keeper during the second half!

As East End were relocating, Our Boys were busily engaged in improving and upgrading the facilities at West Craigie. By the time the 1883/84 season got under way, the club had fully enclosed their ground, and marked the occasion by hosting a highly successful five-a-side tournament; the first time the game of five-a-side football had ever been played in Dundee.

The 'Boys' started the new season well, and after disposing of local rivals West End by the odd-goal-in-five in the first round of the Scottish Cup, they travelled up the coast to take on old adversaries Arbroath at Gayfield in the first round of the new county competition.

A huge travelling support made their way to Arbroath by train and by horse-drawn carriage, such was the interest in the first Forfarshire Cup tie played by either side. The result was that a new record crowd for Gayfield, in excess of 4,000, was recorded.

Although Our Boys started the game well, Arbroath were playing with the advantage of a strong wind at their backs, and scored twice in quick succession to establish a commanding lead which they held until half-time.

In the second half, Our Boys failed to capitalize on the same wind advantage, and the home side put the tie beyond doubt with a further two goals against a single counter from Our Boys to knock the Dundee side out of the competition.

East End, on the other hand, were making their mark in the Forfarshire Cup. Following on from their resounding victory over Dundee Hibernians in the opening round, the MadeiraPark men faced Seafield in round two and progressed to the quarter-final thanks to victory by the odd-goal-in-five. Their reward was a meeting with old adversaries Strathmore.

A large crowd assembled at Strathmore's Rollo's Pier, on Saturday 3rd November 1883, to decide who was to progress to the semi-finals, but unfortunately East End were forced to play with only nine men after two players failed to turn up. Not surprisingly, the home side won comfortably by three goals to nil.

The following month, just days before Christmas, the very first Forfarshire Cup Final was played out between Arbroath and Dundee Harp at Rollo's Pier. Despite incessant rain, a new record crowd for a football match in Dundee of almost 5,000 was recorded, with a good proportion of the spectators having travelled down from Arbroath.

The match itself, however, although keenly contested by both sides, was not the spectacle that had been hoped for, with little good football on display due to the inclement weather. The subsequent report in the following Monday's edition of the Dundee Courier recorded that the ground was *"in a terribly sodden state, the players in frequent parts being over the ankles, while at the close they were scarcely recognisable"*.

When time was called, the score stood in favour of Arbroath by two goals to one, and the players, who were soaked t the skin, gratefully made their way to the relative warmth of the changing room.

It later transpired, however, that the match had been accidentally stopped five minutes early, and a protest was lodged by Harp demanding that the game be replayed.

Their appeal was unsuccessful, and Arbroath became the first team to have their name engraved on the Forfarshire Cup.

Such was the interest in the match, the half-time and full-time scores had been telegraphed to Arbroath from Dundee, where a large crowd had assembled at the local newspaper offices awaiting the outcome. When the final score in favour of Arbroath was announced, *"the cheering could have been heard all over the bounds of the burgh"*, according to the Dundee Courier, who also expressed the opinion that: *"no telegram had given so much universal satisfaction since the fall of Sebastopol was definitely announced"*.

Meanwhile, Our Boys made up for going out in the first round of the Forfarshire Cup to the eventual winners by progressing to last eighteen of the Scottish Cup. After having disposed of West End in the first round, the 'Boys' were drawn to face Arbroath Strathmore at West Craigie Park in round two, where *"a large and enthusiastic concourse of spectators"* endured the blustery conditions to cheer on their favourites to a 2-0 victory.

In the third round of the national competition, just a week after warming up for the tie with an 8-1 thumping of East End, Our Boys lined up to face Strathmore at Rollo's Pier on 20th October 1883. In perfect weather conditions, both sides dished up play of *"fast character"*, in an entertaining match that finished all-square at two goals apiece. Exactly a week later, the two sides met in front of a large and vociferous crowd at West Craigie for the replay, where Our Boys made the most of their home advantage to record a convincing 5-1 victory over their local rivals.

Their reward was a fourth-round trip to Glasgow, to face Pollockshields Athletic on 10th November 1883.

In order to be fresh for the match, the Our Boys players and officials had boarded the 18:40 train from Dundee station on the Friday evening, along with their counterparts from Harp, who were due to play a Scottish Cup tie against Vale of Leven in Alexandria.

After spending the night at a hotel in Glasgow, Our Boys lined up to face Pollockshields at their Hagg's Castle ground, but found the state of the pitch far from ideal. With the underfoot conditions described as being very soft, and with the players *"having sometimes to work in water far above the ankles"*, there was never going to be any good football played by either side.

Pollockshields Athletic, who were obviously more used to the conditions, raced to a six-nil lead before half-time. It was more of the same in the second half and, when the final whistle eventually blew, the home side had scored eleven goals without reply.

Harp fared little better in their cup-tie against Vale of Leven, and their 6-0 reverse, along with Our Boys' heavy defeat, signalled the end of the Dundee clubs' involvement in the national cup competition for another year.

Meanwhile, at MadeiraPark, East End were unfortunately suffering at the hands of the local youths, who had started to use their ground as a playground in the evenings, inflicting damage on the club's facilities. In desperation, secretary Smart was forced in November 1883 to post the following Public Notice in the local press:

"EAST END FOOTBALL CLUB. NOTICE IS HEREBY GIVEN, that after this date, 27th Nov 1883, any Person or Persons other than Members of the aforesaid Club, found playing Football on the Ground belonging the Club, which is known by the name of Madeira

Park, will be prosecuted according to the utmost rigour of the law. By Order the Committee, R. SMART, Secy."

Both the national and county competitions may have been over for Our Boys and East End as the end of the year approached, but both clubs kept interest alive amongst their supporters by organising challenge matches against quality opposition from other parts of the country.

Matters both on and off the field of play were improving steadily now for East End, and home games at MadeiraPark were attracting sizeable attendances. One notable home match played towards the end of 1883 was against Stirling side King's Park, which resulted in a draw of two-goals-apiece. As was often the case back in the early days of Association football, visiting clubs from other areas who visited for friendly games were welcomed with open arms, and were treated as important guests. The report on the King's Park match that appeared in the following Monday's edition of the Dundee Courier describes how the game had been played in the best of spirits and how, after the match, both teams retired to a local hostelry, where pleasantries were exchanged:

"The game was exceedingly pleasant, nothing occurring to mar its harmony, and altogether it was admitted a more hotly contested match has not been played at MadeiraPark. After the match the home team entertained the strangers in the Dundee Arms Inn. Mr Alexander Gow, President of the East End, occupied the chair. The health of 'The Strangers' was drunk with great enthusiasm. McLay (one of the King's Park half-backs), *in reply, wished to give expression to the pleasure his team felt in visiting Dundee, and hoped it would not be the last time they would play in 'Juteopolis'. After spending a pleasant hour together the strangers left with the 6.40 p.m. train".*

Both Our Boys and East End kept the momentum going as far as organising 'crowd-pullers' was concerned when they announced that they had attracted highly reputable Scottish clubs to Dundee for their respective festive holiday programmes in January 1884.

East End announced two matches at Madeira Park; firstly against Glasgow side Dean Park on New Year's Day 1884, followed on 2nd January by a visit from the highly-respected Dunbartonshire side Renton.

Renton had raised a few eyebrows and gained a reputation for themselves earlier in the season when they knocked holders Dumbarton out of the Scottish Cup in the first round, and it was widely anticipated that a bumper crowd would line the ropes at Madeira Park for that particular game.

In the first match, despite putting up a good fight against Dean Park, East End were made to work hard against a fitter side, and went down by four goals to two. It was a tired team, therefore, that lined up to face Renton the following day, and the visitors showed no mercy by rattling home six goals in the first half, during which they had the advantage of the slope. It was more of the same during the second half, and in the end the home side were relieved to hear the final whistle not long after Renton had registered goal number ten.

At West Craigie, Our Boys began the year with a double-header, with Our Boys Rangers, the club's second eleven, facing Glasgow Thornton at noon, followed by Our Boys against Glasgow Northern at 2pm. The second string did the club proud, and held their more fancied opponents to a 1-1 draw, but sadly the main event of the afternoon turned out to be a huge disappointment for the regular patrons at West Craigie. In front of a large crowd, Glasgow Northern, playing uphill during the first half, scored an incredible five goals in as many minutes. Our Boys had no answer to the 'aggressive' play of the visitors, and when the final whistle eventually sounded the home 'keeper had been beaten no fewer than eleven times! The following day, Our Boys faced Greenock Morton at West Craigie, where an improved performance saw the home side lose by the much less embarrassing score of five goals to three.

Early in the 1884, the Forfarshire Football Association announced that an inter-county match had been arranged between Forfarshire and Fifeshire, and the players who had been selected from the various member clubs were announced.

In complete contrast to the previously mentioned sporting attitude displayed by East End President Alexander Gow at the soiree which had followed his club's friendly against King's Park just a few weeks earlier, his sportsmanship was found to be somewhat lacking when he vociferously objected to the team selection for the forthcoming match, stating that certain East End players had been overlooked.

Mr. Gow did not hold back in a letter submitted to the Evening Telegraph, which prompted a huge row:

"After reading over the names, one is forced to the conclusion that it has made a perfect muddle. The Association seems to lack energy and judgment. What was its qualification test? It must have been very low; for it has more scum than cream in its teams. Crack and efficient players have been left out, and novices put forward".

The letter concluded by questioning the sanity of the members of the Association who, it implied, were predominantly affiliated to the Strathmore club, and who had probably put forward the name of every Strathmore player! In Mr. Gow's opinion, the Association had clearly chosen inferior Strathmore men at the expense of better players from East End and Arbroath:

"Did the Strathmore representatives propose all their own men? If they did, they had a daring audacity. The East End and Arbroath had no chance. They are below zero when compared with the immortal Strathmore. According to the Association, Kennedy, of the East End, is only a third-rate goalkeeper. What a piece of mockery. An Association of football lunatics would have known better".

Strong words indeed, and the East End President ruffled more than a few feathers with his outburst, resulting in several angry replies subsequently appearing in the Telegraph columns, including an angry letter from Strathmore Secretary, Marshall Henry:

"though I had nominated every member of the Strathmore team for a place, I do not see that my doing so would lay me open to the charge of "daring audacity" put forth by Mr Gow". "The Strathmore have two members on this Committee, and so have the East End, and it must be apparent to even Mr. Gow that two members of a particular Club cannot elect any person they desire".

The heated debate ensued over the following days, and the correspondence that appeared in the Telegraph's letters page came from contributors who, wishing to remain anonymous, signed themselves off under various nom-de-plumes.

Eventually, Forfarshire Association Vice-President W. E. Buchan was forced to express, in a rather eloquent but tongue-in-cheek manner, his summing up of the entire farcical argument:

"As one of the poor victims who for the past week have had to undergo the torment of passing the keen, though crude, dissecting knife our candid prophetic, but I hope friendly critic, Mr. Gow, I trust that you will grant me a corner for a few observations on his style of handling his victims.

Sir, how in the name of intellect does he expect that any of the humble, ignorant, and "insane" members of said Committee could have the "audacity" to tilt against such a hydra-headed phalanx of literary ability as your football readers will recognise under the sobriquets of "Trams," "Polomus" and the gentle Alec himself.

Why, sir, the idea is absurd, especially when one takes into consideration that Alec has the prophetic power of a member of the Fourth party, the eloquence of O'Connell's Dublin fish vendor, and the refined language of Lord Randolph Churchill".

Eventually, following a debate that raged on for over a week, the matter concluded with the following amusing contribution by an Arbroath correspondent writing under the name of 'Pint Stoup' who, it would appear, was arguing the case for Alexander Gow and the players who had been overlooked by the selection committee:

"I think the Executive has now won for itself a fame which ought not to be allowed to fade away, unwept, unhonoured, and unsung. The Forfarshire Challenge Cup and the Peruvian Mummy have been the means of causing an enormous influx of visitors to the ArbroathMuseum. I understand that room can still be had for further interesting additions, and if a generous football public could arrange to have the Committee embalmed, "cased," and placed alongside one cup, it would be safe to predict such a stream of customers to the "curiosity shop" as would gladden the hearts of the Directorate for many a day".

In spite of this altercation, however, there could be no doubt that the formation of the Forfarshire Football Association just over a year earlier had made a huge impact on Association football in Dundee and the surrounding area, and its inception could only be for the good of the game.

7

The Burns Charity Cup

Competitive football was kept alive during the latter part of the 1883/84 season with the introduction of a charity tournament organised by the Dundee Burns Club, for which a handsome trophy, described as being *"fully equal to the county trophy"*, was procured. The teams competing for the new cup were the big four of Our Boys, East End, Strathmore and Harp; along with West End, who were rapidly establishing themselves as one of the top clubs in Dundee.

The first Burns Charity Cup tie to be played was between East End and Harp at the latter's Viewforth ground on Saturday 2nd February 1883, where East End exited the tournament following a heavy 6-1 defeat. Harp's reward was a home meeting with Our Boys in the semi-final, with Strathmore and West End paired together in the other tie.

Our Boys and Harp warmed up for their cup tie with a challenge match at West Craigie later that month in front of over 5,000 spectators, described as *"the largest assemblage of spectators which has ever turned out to any football contest in Dundee"*. An entertaining match ended in favour of the 'Irishmen' by the odd-goal-in-five, but unfortunately the game was marred by what appears to have been the first hint of sectarianism between two Dundee football teams, to which the reporter from the Dundee Courier lamented:

"It is to be regretted that so much feeling, apparently of a national character, should have been imported into the contest, and that occasionally at trying moments unhallowed hands were laid on opposing players by one or two members of both teams."

Despite this apparent ill-feeling, however, the players and officials from both sides made their way to a local hostelry after the match, where they *"spent a pleasant hour together with song and sentiment"*.

On Saturday 6th April 1884, the same two sides lined up against each other in their eagerly-anticipated Burns Charity Cup semi-final at Harp's Viewforth ground. Conditions were perfect for football, and yet another record crowd turned out to witness the event, with the gate receipts of over £90 indicating an attendance of around 7,000. As the kick-off approached, the scene both inside and outside the ground (which was located on the north side of the Perth Road, near its junction with Hawkhill), is described in great detail by an article which appeared in a subsequent edition of the Evening Telegraph:

"Harp's ground at Viewforth was literally packed in every nook and cranny with an eager and expectant crowd. Trees, dyke heads, and even housetops were quickly seized upon by the more enthusiastic and venturesome of the onlookers, while one individual might have been seen swaying gently to and fro in the scanty branches of a slender sapling.

The Harp were first to enter the field, and were loudly cheered by their supporters as they appeared arrayed in new jerseys, on the left breast of which were sewn, in bright yellow and of very perceptible proportions, counterparts of the instrument from which the Club derive their name.

A few minutes later Our Boys appeared, amidst a burst of applause, attired in the more sombre dark blue. Of the two teams the green jerseys seemed the more confident previous to the start, but when the field was set and the ball kicked off it was soon apparent that every player on the ground meant business".

It was Our Boys who exerted the early pressure, however, and deservedly took the lead after just a few minutes' play despite playing up the slope.

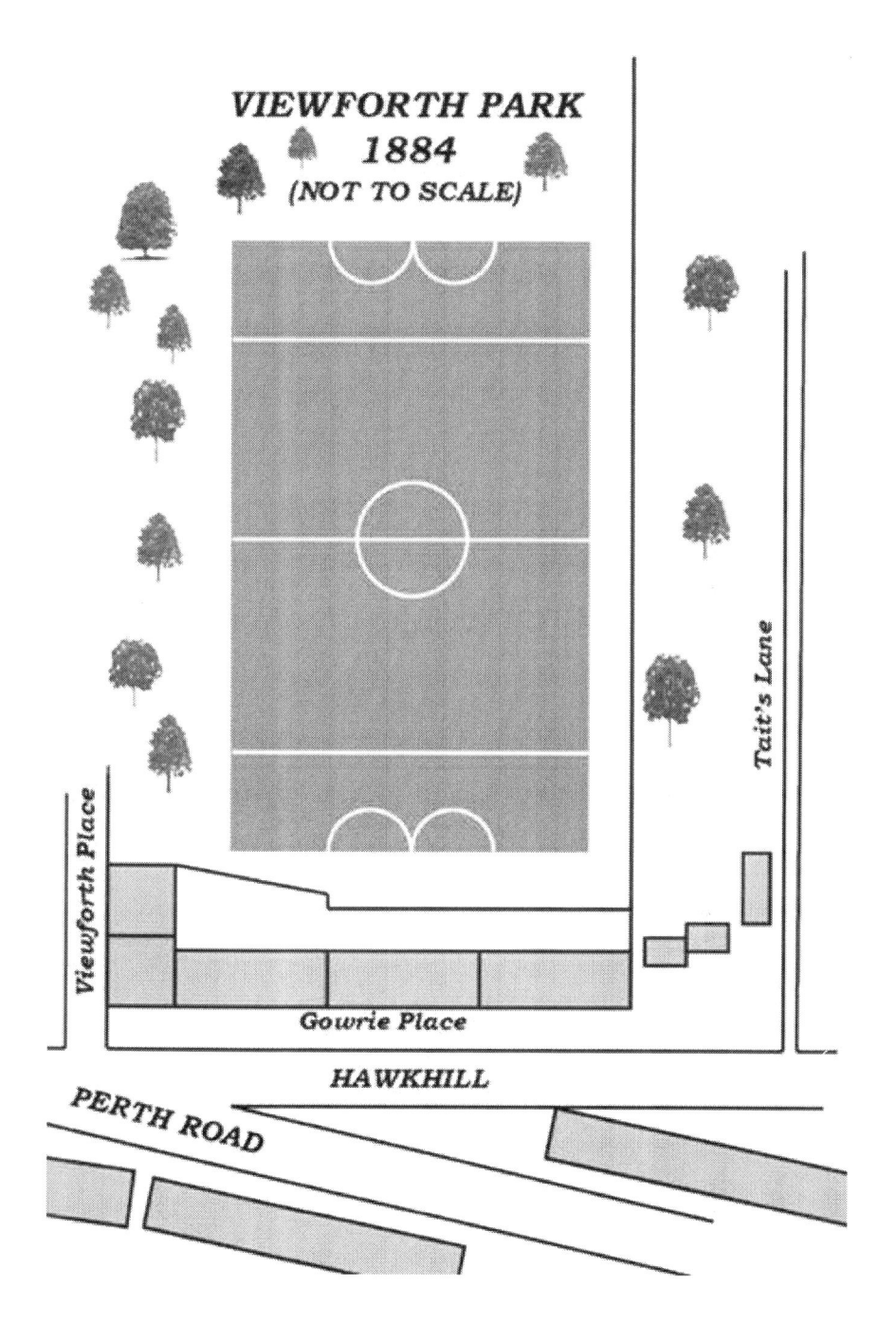

Harp's Viewforth Park, where a crowd of 7,000 witnessed the semi-final of the Burns Charity Cup in April 1884

Although the dark-blues managed to maintain pressure on the home goal, they found the Harp 'keeper in great form, and failed to capitalise on their superiority. Eventually, just before the interval, Harp scored the equaliser amidst wild cheering from the home supporters, which was allowed to stand despite strong claims of offside from Our Boys.

The pace of the game was stepped up after the interval, and with it came an element of rough play from both sides. It was the Harp who eventually gained the upper hand, however, and scored twice to establish a 3-1 lead before Our Boys, who were starting to show signs of tiredness as the match wore on, scored what turned out to be a consolation goal. The match eventually ended 3-2 in favour of the home side.

The local press, whilst conceding that the game had been an exciting one, also expressed concern that the match had been played out in such a rough manner, and stated:

"It is to be regretted that discreditable ebullitions of temper on the part of individual players occasionally disfigured the game, and on one occasion, I hear, a player received a rather severe blow from an opponent. The Association could surely find means, if an act of this description can be proved against any player, of dealing summarily with the offender, as no circumstances whatever can justify a player in resorting to conduct of this sort".

Unfortunately, the local residents were also caught up in the aftermath, with several householders reporting damage to property caused by spectators climbing on to the roofs of the houses in Gowrie Place, at the southern end of Viewforth Park. The damage was eventually made good at the expense of the Burns Charity Fund.

Subsequent protests were lodged by Our Boys on the grounds that Harp's first goal had been offside, and that the dimensions of their Viewforth ground were *"less than the minimum limit sanctioned by the Association"*. The protests were thrown out, and Harp progressed to the final.

Our Boys refused to let the matter rest, however, and vented their frustration by withdrawing from the Forfarshire Football Association, the governing body responsible for organising the Burns Charity Cup competition. The West Craigie Park club would now, unless they had a change of heart, take no further part in any tournament organised by the Forfarshire Association, including the Forfarshire Cup and the Burns Charity Cup.

It was generally agreed that, with the best two sides in Dundee having been drawn together in the semi-final played out at Viewforth, the winners of this tie would be the eventual winners of the Burns Charity Cup. Harp proved this opinion to be correct at the end of the month when they swept West End aside by seven goals without reply in a rather one-sided final at Strathmore's Rollo's Pier.

Despite having suffered some disappointing results over the course of the 1883/84 campaign, Our Boys were reported to be growing from strength to strength as the season reached a conclusion. The club now boasted a membership of 170 compared to only 76 the previous year, and Our Boys could also be content that they had won far more matches than they had lost, along with a favourable goals tally.

East End, too, were happy to report that they were in a healthy position as a football club, boasting a membership just short of one hundred. On the field of play, their season had also been reasonably satisfactory, with a total of 27 matches played; ten of which had been won, ten lost, and seven drawn.

Unfortunately, East End once again found themselves homeless, when it was announced that the proposed Dundee Suburban Railway (which ironically was never built!) was to cut through MadeiraPark from Pitkerro Road to Forfar Road. Presumably, in order to prepare the land for sale to the railway company, the land owners terminated the club's rental agreement.

Consequently, East End were forced to start looking for yet another home ground. They kicked off the 1884/85 season ground sharing with Strathmore at Rollo's Pier, where they thumped Coupar Angus 8-1 in the first round of the Scottish Cup in mid-September. A good start was also made in the Forfarshire Cup, with a 5-0 away victory recorded against Windmill.

By early October, the club had secured a ground not far from their former MadeiraPark home, situated adjacent to the west wall of BaxterPark, immediately to the north of Our Boys' WestCraigiePark. The new ground, which was christened PitkerroPark, was opened on 11th October 1884 with a Scottish Cup second round replay against Strathmore, a week after the two sides had drawn 1-1 at Rollo's Pier. However, the conditions that greeted the teams that afternoon were far from favourable, and good football was never going to be possible.

Heavy rain had fallen before kick-off, which made the playing surface extremely slippery, and by the time the match got under way the wind had risen to gale-force, blowing down the park from north to south, accompanied by more torrential rain. Playing down the ground's bad slope with the wind at their backs, East End piled on the pressure during the first half, and the ball seemed to be permanently in the vicinity of the south goal, but the home side only managed to score twice before half-time.

Strathmore enjoyed the same wind and slope advantage during the second half and beat East End 'keeper Kennedy on five occasions, but fully twenty minutes before the game was scheduled to finish, the referee decided to call a halt to proceedings due to the inclement weather. The score line when the match was abandoned stood 5-2 in favour of Strathmore and, as this lead was deemed to have been out of East End's reach at the time, it was allowed to stand as the final result!

Meanwhile, immediately to the south of PitkerroPark in adjoining WestCraigiePark, Our Boys were playing host to Cowdenbeath in a friendly, where exactly the same scenario unfolded. With the score standing at two goals apiece at the end of the first half, Our Boys took full advantage of the wind after the half-time interval and rattled home six goals in the space of half-an-hour. However, as had happened in the East End v Strathmore match, the referee decided to call a halt to proceedings with Our Boys leading 8-2, when *"a deluge of rain, accompanied by a hurricane of wind, came on"*, forcing the players to return to the dressing room drenched to the skin as the crowd quickly dispersed and hurried home to their firesides.

Sadly, the conditions were to have far reaching consequences for East End goalkeeper William Kennedy. By all accounts the custodian had taken to the field already suffering from illness, and the cold and wet conditions caused his condition to deteriorate rapidly. Just over two weeks later, local football circles were shocked and saddened to learn that the player had passed away at home. Following his funeral, on 1st November 1884, the Evening Telegraph lamented:

"So Saturday saw the last of poor Kennedy. His funeral was attended by many of his comrades in the East End, and the Club had furnished a wreath as a last token of affection. One of the best custodians in the 'shire, Kennedy was a keen lover of the game, and almost to the end his enthusiasm remained. His death, accelerated by a severe chill caught while engaged at his favourite pastime, at the early age of twenty-seven, will be widely regretted in football circles, where in life he was much liked".

Following the exit from the Scottish Cup at the hands of Strathmore, and the mournful demise of their goalkeeper, East End's season went from bad to worse. In only the second match played at PitkerroPark, the home side suffered an even more humiliating defeat, this time from Arbroath by ten-goals-to-three in the second round of the Forfarshire Cup.

There can be no doubt the club was missing the presence of goalkeeper Kennedy, and it was abundantly clear that an air of despondency had descended on the club. Having also been knocked out of both the Scottish Cup and the Forfarshire Cup in the early rounds, everyone associated with East End had little appetite for the game in the weeks that followed.

Our Boys, on the other hand, were going through a purple patch. In the first round of the Scottish Cup, a resounding 4-1 win over Arbroath Strathmore at the latter's Damley Park secured a second round home meeting with West End. In front of a big crowd at West Craigie, which consisted largely of vociferous sets of supporters from both clubs, who *"gave frequent manifestations of their feelings as the game progressed"*, Our Boys completely overwhelmed their local rivals to cruise into round three with an 8-1 victory.

Their reward was another home tie against local rivals Strathmore, who were successfully overcome with yet another convincing score-line, although by all accounts the game was not as one-sided as the final result might suggest. During the opening exchanges the visitors looked the more dangerous and, with the slope to their advantage, deservedly took the lead after just five minutes.

This early reverse gave the home side a rude awakening, and before half-time they had built up a commanding 3-1 lead. Although the second half was evenly contested, Our Boys scored two late goals to win by the somewhat undeserved final tally of five-goals-to-one.

Round four of the national competition saw Our Boys drawn at home to West Benhar, who hailed from a mining community near Harthill in North Lanarkshire. On 15th November 1884 at West Craigie, in *"favourable weather"*, a large crowd gathered to witness the action, and they were not to be disappointed.

Despite slippery underfoot conditions, both sides played entertaining football and, *"amidst hearty cheering"*, two goals were scored in the opening five minutes, one for each side. When half-time was called, both teams had registered a second goal.

In the second half, both sides went at each other hammer-and-tongs, with several chances created at either end of the park. According to one match report, *"the ball travelled rapidly from goal to goal"*, so it was rather surprising that there was no further scoring; the match eventually finishing all-square at two goals apiece.

Exactly a week later, Our Boys made the long five-hour journey by train from Dundee through to Shotts, which was the closest point to Benhar's ground that could be reached on the railway network.

With the North Lanarkshire club having incredibly remained unbeaten in their last seventy home outings, the Dundee lads knew they were in for a tough time, but nobody expected what lay in store when the team and officials alighted at Shotts railway station.

Our Boys had expected a reception committee, but there was no club official waiting to greet the team, nor was there any transport available to convey them the considerable distance to the football ground. Instead, the players and officials had to work out which route to take and, after having initially set off in the wrong direction, had to walk, carrying their kit, over five miles along a rough *"furnace slag road"*.

The party eventually arrived at their final destination tired and weary, and the match got under way just as darkness was starting to fall. Several players were forced to take to the field suffering from blisters, whilst others complained of cramp, and it came as no surprise when the home side scored three times in the opening minutes to take control of the game.

Although the Dundee lads tried their best, they eventually succumbed to defeat by eight goals to three, and their Scottish Cup campaign was over for another season.

It was now all too apparent why the North Lanarkshire side had remained unbeaten at home for so long. Visiting sides were simply not in a fit state to play football on arrival at West Benhar after having had to trek five-miles from the railway station to the ground!

Our Boys subsequently lodged a protest against West Benhar on the grounds that they had been treated inhospitably, and that their pre-arranged transport from Shotts to Harthill had not been provided. Their appeal fell on deaf ears.

Whilst Our Boys were enjoying their successful run in the Scottish Cup, East End's prospects of ending their poor run of performances were boosted when it was announced in December 1884 that the club was to merge with local rivals Victoria F.C., a club that had only been founded the previous year. The Victoria players had proved their worth earlier in the campaign when they recorded a resounding 7-0 victory over Perseverance in the Forfarshire Cup, and this much-needed injection of fresh skill re-kindled some much-needed enthusiasm in East End F.C.

The first game to be played following the amalgamation was a friendly with Strathmore at Rollo's Pier on Saturday 13th December and, although East End lost by the odd-goal-in-five, the team came in for much praise from the local press, who were of the opinion that it would only be a matter of time before the club regained its former status. That opinion was vindicated when, on New Year's Day 1885, East End played host to Glasgow side Springburn at PitkerroPark, where they recorded an astounding 7-2 victory. It now looked very much like East End were finally about to re-establish themselves as a side to be reckoned with. Or was more trouble lurking just around the corner?

8

A Hooligan Element Starts to Creep In

Meanwhile, as everyone connected with East End were desperately trying to keep their club afloat, Our Boys' continued success was drawing an increasing number of spectators to home games and, towards the end of 1884, further improvements were carried out at West Craigie, including the erection of a grandstand running parallel to the west touch line. Described as being *"of a most substantial character"*, the new stand was capable of seating 500 spectators on eight rows of bench seats, who would now be able to enjoy *"a splendid view of the whole playing area"*.

The new grandstand was opened on Saturday 13th December 1884 for a friendly against Bo'ness, the holders of the Edinburgh Consolation Cup, and the home side emerged victors by three goals without reply. A large crowd turned out in *"highly favourable"* weather for the match, and by all accounts the new stand was well patronised; the spectators within the new facility being happy to part with an additional 3d (1½ p) on top of their usual 3d admission charge for the privilege of having a seat.

For their New Year programme of matches, Our Boys played host to the famous Dunbartonshire club Renton on the first of January 1885 at West Craigie, where the new grandstand was filled to overflowing. An additional 4,000 spectators were crammed in to the other three sides of the enclosure.

The reason for such interest in this match was that Renton had, just six days earlier, knocked Rangers out of the Scottish Cup by five goals to three at the quarter-final stage,

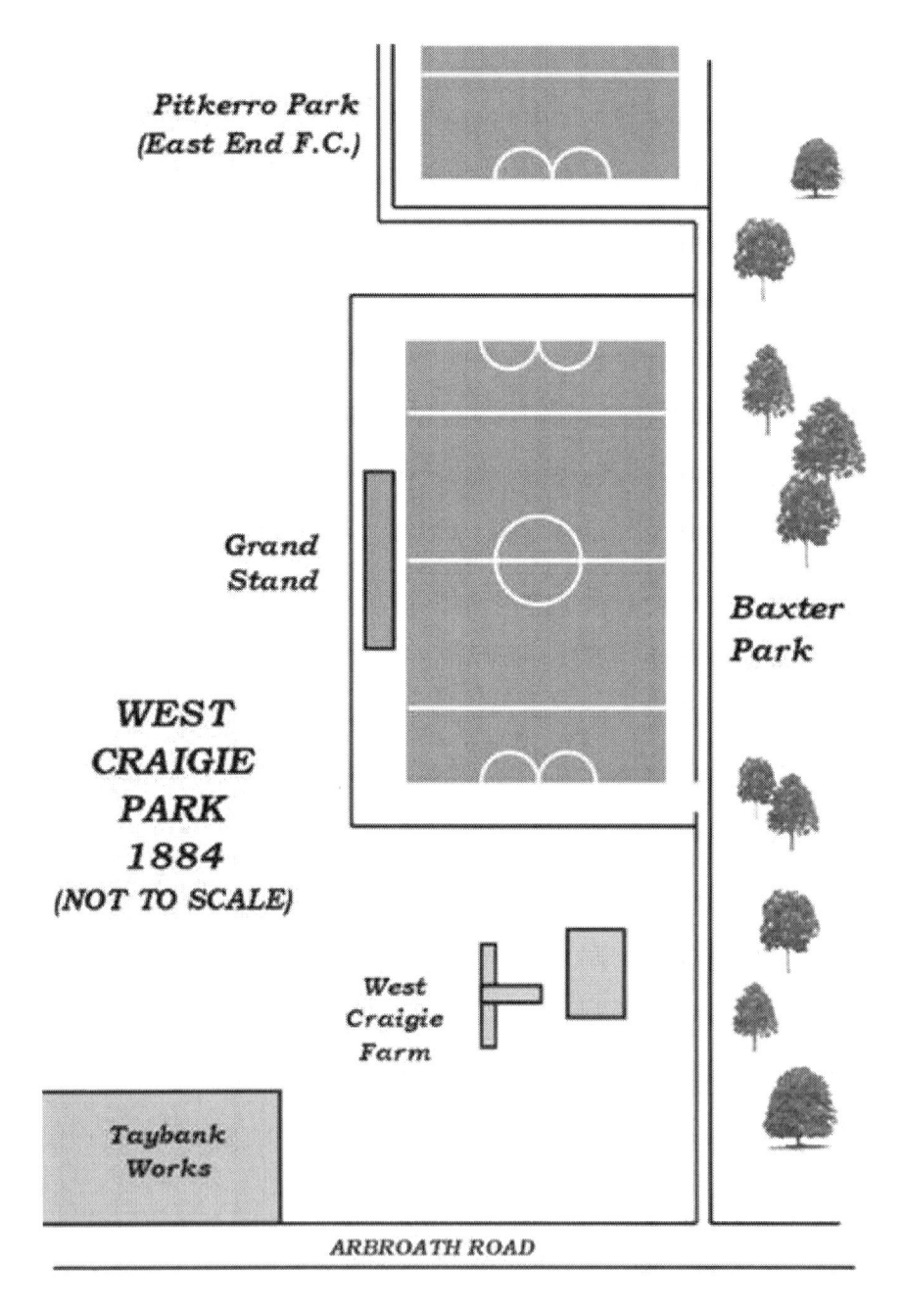

West Craigie Park in 1884, after the construction of the ground's first grandstand.

and the Dundee public were no doubt keen to see for themselves the skills of the visiting side.

Renton more than lived up to expectations, and although the result was a trifle disappointing for the home side, the crowd were treated to a *"brilliant passing game"* by the visitors, who won convincingly by nine-goals-to-one. However, it has to be said that Our Boys' luck deserted them in front of goal, and they had, by all accounts, matched their opponents for lengthy periods throughout the match. For the record, Renton went on to beat Hibernian just over three weeks later in the semi-final of the Scottish Cup before going on to lift the trophy thanks to a 3-1 replay victory over Vale of Leven at Hampden.

The following day, a weakened Our Boys side played host to Partick Thistle in front of another large crowd, and were unfortunate to go down by the odd goal in five, with the visitors scoring the winner with virtually the last kick of the ball.

On Saturday 17th January 1885, the first meeting of the season between Our Boys and East End was played at West Craigie, but unfortunately there wasn't much in the way of good football on display. With the underfoot conditions described as 'sodden', both teams had difficulty in keeping their feet, with the result that towards the end of the match the players of both sides were barely recogniseable, being covered from head to foot in mud. It was the home side that adapted best to the conditions, however, and the resurgent East End's confidence was dealt a severe blow with a six-nil defeat. It would appear that thePitkerroPark side were going to have to live in the shadow of their near-neighbours for the time being at least!

During the early months of 1885 it became apparent from reports in the local press that a hooligan element was starting to manifest itself within a small section of Our Boys' support. Unruly behaviour at West Craigie was first reported following a match against Glasgow Northern on 24th January, when the Evening Telegraph commented:

"The game was not so agreeable as one could have wished. The Northern, judging from the manifestations of a number of the spectators, do not seem to be at all favourites with a portion of the frequenters of WestCraigiePark. It is a pity that this nuisance of hostile demonstrations outside the ropes, which is becoming far too common at all our grounds, could not be greatly modified, or, what is better, given up altogether. They serve no purpose whatever, except to render disagreeable to the bulk of the onlookers many a good game. It is to be hoped the hint will not be thrown away".

It would appear that the Telegraph's appeal to those responsible was not heeded. Just a week later, unruly scenes at the end of Our Boys' 5-4 victory over Strathmore at Rollo's Pier, during which referee Mr J.S. Gibson of West End F.C. was allegedly assaulted, prompted an angry response from the official concerned.

In a strongly worded letter to the press on Monday 2nd February 1885, Mr Gibson claimed that a faction of Our Boys' supporters had invaded the field at the end of the match and pelted him with mud and stones, forcing him to take cover. The official then alleged that, when he had started to make his way home after he thought the unruly mob had dispersed, he was met by the same crowd, who *"indulged in hooting and yelling all along the Perth Road and Nethergate, occasionally varying the proceedings by throwing mud"*. Mr Gibson then concluded by expressing the opinion that *"from henceforth all gentlemen will be conspicuous by their absence from Our Boys' matches"*.

The response from Our Boys was immediate. In a letter to the Dundee Courier on the following day from club secretary G. A. Duncan, the unruly behaviour of the 'West Craigie supporters' was emphatically denied, and the match official's impartiality was called into question. Mr Duncan then went on to say that, in actual fact, the Our Boys' officials and players had done all they could *"to protect Mr Gibson from the resentment of the crowd"*.

The Our Boys secretary did, however, hint that Mr Gibson had only himself to blame for *"such unwonted display of feeling "*, and questioned the referee's ideas of fair play!

The match official refused to let the matter rest, and submitted a further letter to the same newspaper, claiming to have evidence to the contrary regarding our Boys' version of events:

"Sir, - I regret troubling you with another letter on this disagreeable subject. It will probably be food for reflection to Mr Duncan to have the following evidence in support of the facts stated in my last letter. When his friends commenced their "deplorable" conduct Mr Duncan was within ten feet of me, but before twenty seconds had elapsed he had removed as many yards away. This was the support and protection afforded me by him and all the other officials of Our Boys. One of the Strathmore players was chased across the field, and another was kicked and struck, and surely this proves to the most ordinary intellect which of the clubs' partisans indulged in lawless conduct. Finally, when going home, I was escorted by four of the Strathmore Club, who duly received a share of the mud flying around, and if this be the way approved of at West Craigie by which supporters show their appreciation of a team, I cannot regret that it is not relished in other quarters.

Yours truly, J. S. Gibson, West End F. C".

Now it was Our Boys' turn to retaliate to Mr Gibson's strongly worded accusations, and two letters subsequently appeared in the Courier's letters column.

The first, from club secretary Duncan, accused the match official of having imagined the facts stated in his correspondence, before implying that:

"Mr. Gibson is as great an adept at mud-throwing as is a Rollo's Pier crowd".

The second letter, from Our Boys' goalkeeper Philip Ovenstone, also accused the referee of falsifying the evidence, stating:

"Mr. Gibson's memory must have failed him or he would not have replied as he did, for when he was assailed by the crowd of youngsters as he was leaving the field I went between him and his assailants and stopped the abuse till he got into the dressing-room; and had he asked, or even waited till we were dressed, instead of ignoring us, he would have got the same protection afforded him on his road home".

And there, finally, the aftermath of that particular incident was put to rest. However, as the old proverb says, 'there's no smoke without fire', and it has to be said that there probably was, at the time, a certain hooligan element manifesting itself within the regular patrons of Our Boys Football Club.

Meanwhile, East End's fortunes on the field of play were slowly improving. Discounting the aforementioned 6-0 defeat the hands of Our Boys in atrocious conditions in January, the PitkerroPark side's performances had been improving steadily following their amalgamation with Victoria, and victories included a 3-1 away victory over West End at the beginning of February.

This was followed up with an incredible 6-6 draw with Strathmore at Pitkerro Park; a *"fierce and exciting contest"* that East End would have won had it not been for an early injury to their 'keeper, who had to play out the remainder of the match with one of his legs heavily strapped up.

"The East End played with a vigorous determination that could not be resisted" commented the reporter from the Dundee Courier, who concluded: *"The East End played to a man. Every member of the team showed splendid form"*.

With such praise being heaped on the side, everyone associated with the club had good reason to feel confident about the future. Unfortunately, however, East End were then dealt yet another blow when it transpired they were once again having to endure the heartache of being rendered homeless.

Their landlords, the Royal Lunatic Asylum Trustees, had entered into negotiations early in 1885 with a view to selling off the land on which PitkerroPark was situated. In order to make the land more attractive to prospective purchasers, a new road infrastructure was to be constructed, including a road running from west to east, directly through the middle of East End's ground, to connect Albert Street with a new western entrance to BaxterPark.

When East End were evicted to allow construction work on the new road to commence, they went into a state of idleness for two weeks, before returning to action on Saturday 7th March with an impressive 2-1 victory over Arbroath Strathmore at Damley Park.

Meanwhile, the draw for the Burns Charity Cup tournament, organised under the auspices of the Forfarshire Association, went ahead with just four clubs participating, following Our Boys' withdrawal from the Association the previous year.

General feeling in local football circles, however, was that Our Boys should have been included in the competition despite not being members of the F.F.A., as the tournament was organised to aid local charities, and the exclusion of one of Dundee's top teams would obviously have a detrimental effect on monies raised.

To their credit, the West Craigie club generously announced that they would donate a proportion of their gate money from the matches they were due to play on the dates when the charity tournament matches were scheduled.

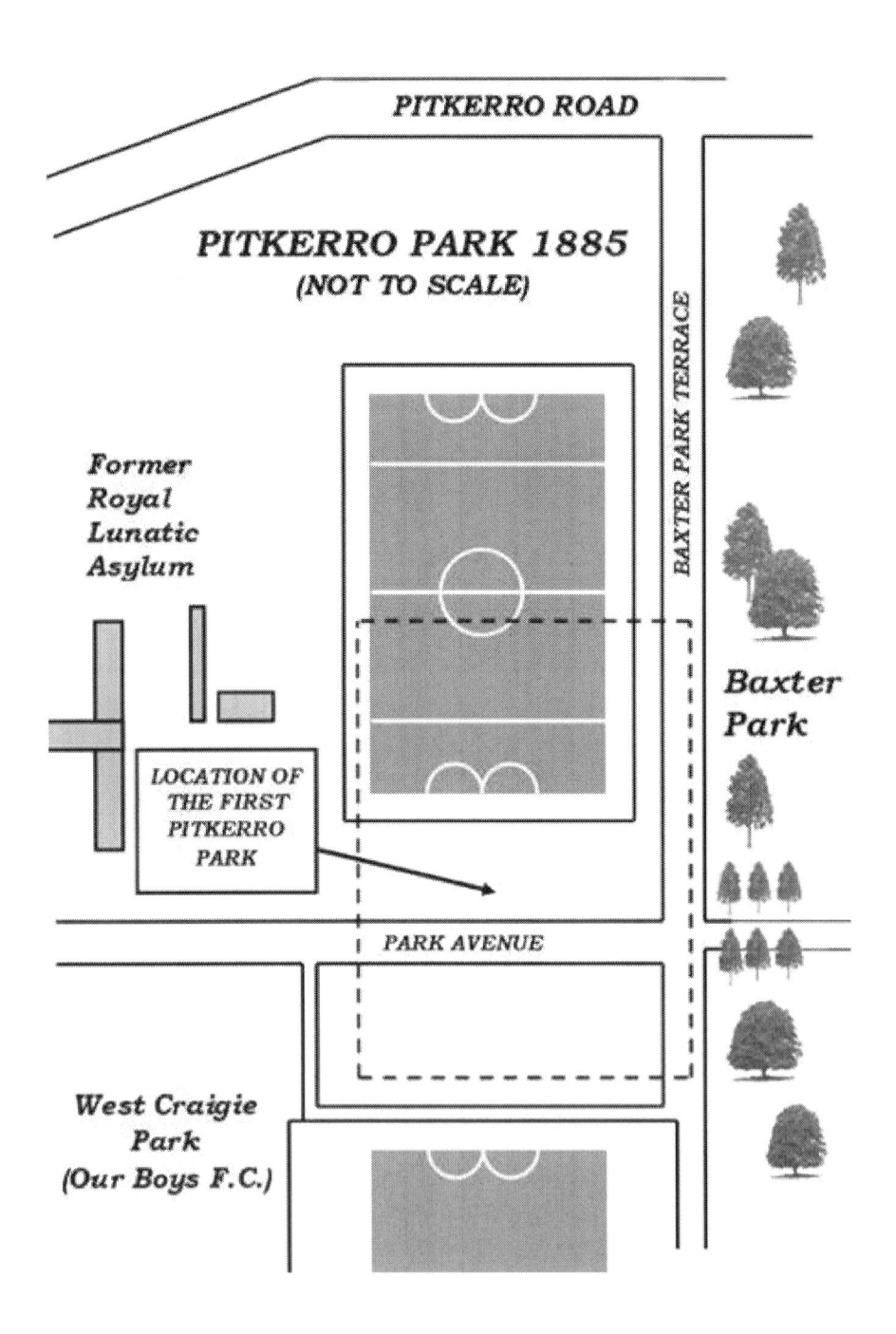

Pitkerro Park in 1885, following construction of the new road infrastructure including Park Avenue and BaxterPark Terrace.

East End were drawn to face the previous season's finalists, West End, with choice of ground, but as they were now homeless, they had no other option but to concede ground rights to their opponents. The match was played on Saturday 21st March at West End's BogheadPark, an exposed ground situated on the north side of Blackness Road, near to its junction with West Park Road.

With a strong westerly wind at their backs, East End took full advantage of the conditions, and continuous pressure on the home defence was eventually rewarded with a goal. When half-time was called, East End were unfortunate not to have increased their lead, with two further goals having been chalked off for alleged infringements.

In the second half, however, the home side held the wind advantage, and with East End also having to contend with playing towards a strong setting sun, it was no surprise when West End levelled the match with a wind assisted effort. There was no further scoring, and the match ended all-square at a goal-apiece.

Determined not to hand their opponents ground advantage for a second time, East End sought out a suitable venue for the replay, and eventually secured the use of Harp's new ground, opened a year previously, which was sandwiched between East Dock Street and Broughty Ferry Road, adjacent to Dundee Gas Works. There, on Saturday 11th April 1885, East End and West End battled it out on a rain-sodden surface.

With a large pool of water having formed in front of the north goal, good play on that part of the park was rendered impossible, and much amusement was had by the 2,000 spectators as players frequently toppled over into the water and were drenched!

It was West End who adapted better to the conditions during the first half, and held a 2-1 lead when half-time was called.

During the second half, however, East End managed to equalise, and eventually won an otherwise uneventful game with a deciding goal five minutes from time.

Two weeks later, East End and Harp lined up at the latter's East Dock Street to contest the final of the Burns Charity Cup, with governing body the Forfarshire Football Association having been unable to secure a neutral venue for the match.

Unfortunately, it turned out to be a disappointing game as far as East End were concerned. Harp were undoubtedly the form team and, playing with home advantage, there was really only going to be one outcome.

As had been the case with the semi-final against West End at the same venue, the underfoot conditions were far from perfect following a deluge of rain earlier in the day, and large puddles of water covered a large part of the surface. Despite the conditions, Harp pressurised the East End goal right from the start, and scored the opener in the opening minute. Before the half-time whistle sounded the home team were three goals to the good.

In the second half, East End gave it their best shot and created several chances, but unfortunately their efforts came to nothing; and, when the referee finally called a halt to proceedings, the Harp were declared victors by six-goals-to-nothing.

There was, however, good news for East End. At the club's annual 'Club Festival and Assembly', which had been held in the Thistle Hall on the eve of the cup final, Chairman Alexander Gow announced that, through the kindness of the landlords of Pitkerro Park, the Asylum Trustees, a suitable piece of ground on which to lay out a new football park had been granted to the club.

This land was just a few yards to the north of their previous ground, and a little closer to Pitkerro Road. East End wasted no time in carrying out the necessary preparations, which in essence were simply a reconstruction of their old ground; and, just over four weeks later, on Tuesday 26th May 1885, the new PitkerroPark was opened with a 2-1 friendly victory over Our Boys.

The club now had every reason to look forward with confidence. In the words of Chairman Gow, East End had, for the last two years, been *"fighting grim adversity"*.

Now, following the amalgamation with Victoria F.C. and the acquisition of a new ground, they had been *"restored to life and vigour again"*. Perseverance and determination was what had steered the club through the difficult times, according to Mr. Gow, and he was confident that the club would eventually *"regain what they had lost."*

East End, due to circumstances out-with their control, had played only seventeen matches throughout the 1884/85 season, of which six had been won, four drawn, and seven lost. Everyone associated with the club were now confident, however, that matters would be turned around sooner rather than later.

Our Boys, having had no involvement in the Charity Cup, went all-out during the latter stages of the 1884/85 season to attract some of the country's best teams to Dundee for challenge matches at WestCraigiePark. Before the season was out, Our Boys had played host to Heart of Midlothian, Hibernian, Rangers, Dumbarton, Cowlairs and Scottish Cup holders Renton to name but a few.

After a proposal to bring Aston Villa north at the beginning of April fell through, Our Boys rounded off their season with a game against Bolton Wanderers at West Craigie, where the first English side to visit Dundee won an exciting game by the odd goal in seven.

At Our Boys' AGM, held in the Reform Street Hall at the end of the season, Chairman Mr. James Dron reported that club was *"in a highly satisfactory condition"*. Like East End, however, the West Craigie side had, over the course of the season, lost more matches than they had won, but the Chairman was quick to point out that the matches lost had been mostly against highly-respected teams, including west of Scotland clubs Renton, Third Lanark, Rangers and Cowlairs, as well as the two big Edinburgh sides, Hibernian and Heart of Midlothian.

Most importantly, however, a proposal that Our Boys should apply to re-join the Forfarshire Football Association was unanimously passed. The future was now looking rosier for Our Boys as well as for East End!

9

Football Fever

By the mid-1880's, there existed what can only be described as 'Football Fever' in the Burgh of Dundee and beyond. Every day the game seemed to be coming more popular. On street corners, groups of men could be seen discussing the various merits of the game. In the factories and workshops, the topic of discussion at meal breaks was now mainly based around how the local sides were faring. The newspapers, too, were caught up in the excitement, and were now devoting several column inches to the game.

Never before had there been a game that had caught the public's imagination in such a way, and its benefits were there for all to see. Hundreds of young men, who might otherwise have wasted their free time indulging in some unhealthy pursuit, were now engaged in improving their physical fitness in order to play the game. Others, who preferred to line the ropes at the various football grounds on Saturday afternoons, were now in the habit of reading newspapers and, in doing so, were either learning to read or were improving their basic literary skills.

In Dundee, local charities were also benefiting from football, with the Burns Charity Cup now providing a much-needed cash injection into local causes. Since its inception, local institutions such as the Royal Infirmary, the Convalescent Home, the Orphan Institution and the local lifeboat had all received a contribution. Generous donations had also been made to local disaster appeals, including aid for those affected by the sinking of the Dundee whaler 'Chieftain', lost near Iceland; and the families of seven men drowned in a boating accident at the mouth of the Tay.

The fortunes East End were also now showing signs of great improvement. Now settled in to their new PitkerroPark home, where they were destined to remain for the next six seasons, they opened their 1885/86 campaign with convincing home victories over Angus (Forfar); Forfar Athletic and West End.

The club then embarked on their best Scottish Cup run to date. On 12th September 1885, the spoils were shared in a 3-3 draw with Strathmore at PitkerroPark in the first round of the national competition, but the home side were aggrieved when what they thought was a late winner was disallowed by the referee. A week later at Rollo's Pier, however, East End got the better of their local rivals with a convincing 4-1 victory to progress to round two.

Following a 2-2 draw with Broughty Ferry in the second round at Pitkerro Park on 3rd October, East End made three changes to their side for the replay at Forthill a week later, and it looked like the move had paid off with a convincing 8-3 victory. However, it later transpired that East End had committed a *"flagrant violation of the registration rule"*, and the S.F.A decreed that the match had to be replayed. The club proved that they were worthy of a place in the third round, however, with a 2-1 victory at the same venue on 17th October.

Just a week later, East End made the trip up the coast to face Arbroath at Gayfield in the third round of the Scottish Cup. The PitkerroPark men had every reason to be apprehensive as they prepared for this tie, as Arbroath had, in the first round of the competition, scored a record 36 goals without reply as they knocked Aberdeen side Bon Accord out of the cup. This remarkable score-line stands to this day as the biggest-ever winning margin in an Association football match, although it was challenged in more recent years by an alleged 149-0 victory by Madagascar side A.S. Adema that was later disproved.

Although East End managed to avoid losing by a margin anything like that suffered by Bon Accord, they were outplayed by a rampant Arbroath side and exited the national competition following a seven-nil reverse.

Incidentally, on the same day that Arbroath recorded their historic 36-0 win, Dundee Harp managed to score 35 goals without reply in their Scottish Cup fixture against Aberdeen Rovers at East Dock Street. In fact, the result of this tie was originally thought to have been 37-0, but it later transpired that the referee had failed to keep an accurate tally of the goals scored and, following an intervention by the Harp officials, the total was reduced by two.

Had it not been for the honesty of Harp, it could well have been the case that it was the Dundee side who now held the record and not Arbroath!

Meanwhile, at West Craigie, Our Boys had also made a good start to the 1885/86 season. After opening with a 4-1 home win against West End, the team had the honour of participating in an exhibition match against a Glasgow Select side, comprised entirely of Queen's Park players, in Perth on 15th August to commemorate the opening of St. Johnstone's *"convenient and commodious"* Recreation Ground, which was located immediately to the west of Perth Prison.

The choice of teams to mark the occasion had been made, by all accounts, in order to demonstrate to the young St. Johnstone players, who were watching the match from the touchlines, how the Association game should be played, as well as giving the local patrons *"an opportunity of witnessing the pastime at its best"*.

A week later, Our Boys treated their own supporters to a thrilling match against Renton, the Scottish Cup holders, and had the visitors not scored a last-minute equaliser a famous victory would have been recorded.

After disposing of Coupar Angus in the first round of the Scottish Cup at the beginning of September, Our Boys were drawn to face Harp in the second round, on Saturday 3rd October 1885 at Harp's East Dock Street.

However, on Saturday 19th September, just a fortnight before the eagerly awaited Scottish Cup tie was due, the same two clubs lined up to face each other at the same venue in the first round of the Forfarshire Cup. Great excitement prevailed in the days and hours leading up to the match and, on the day itself, thousands of supporters of both sides crowded the streets leading to the Harp football ground, over two hours before the scheduled kick-off time of 3:30.

Inside the ground, well before the game was due to begin, there was not an inch of standing room to be had. Harp's newly erected grandstand, which was in use for the first time, was filled to its 1,000 seat capacity. By all accounts, the crowd inside the enclosure numbered between 10,000 and 12,000, many of whom had come from as far away as Perth, Forfar and Arbroath, such was the interest in the match.

This figure did not, of course, include the hundreds of spectators who had found vantage points on the roofs of the adjoining factory buildings on the east side of the ground, nor did it take into account those who watched the match from the windows of the houses in Broughty Ferry Road. It was, nonetheless, a new record crowd for a football match in Dundee.

When the teams took to the field, the atmosphere inside EastDockStreetPark had risen to fever-pitch, and loud cheering greeted the players of both sides. When play got under way, both teams went at it *"hammer and tongs"*, but eventually tempers became frayed, with several players losing control and lashing out with hands and feet at the opposition. According to press reports, the first half contained *"the coarsest football which has ever been witnessed in Dundee"*.

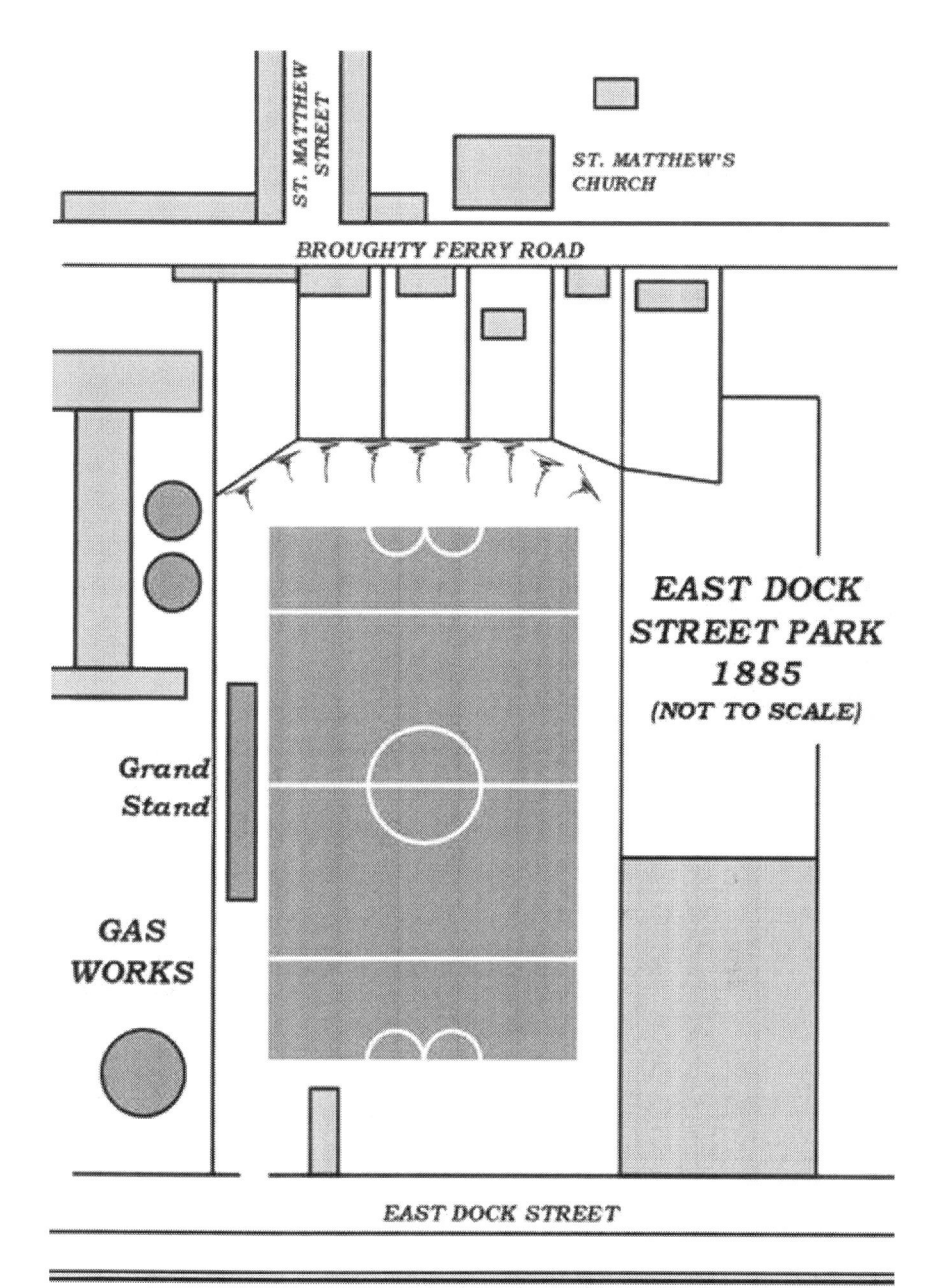

East Dock Street was the home ground of Harp F.C. for ten years from 1884 until the eventual demise of the club in 1894. The grandstand was opened in 1885.

Half-an-hour after the game had started, Harp notched the first goal amidst wild cheering from their followers and, before the half-time whistle sounded, the home side had doubled their advantage, with scenes of jubilation once again erupting amongst the home support.

In the second half, Our Boys tried their hardest to reduce the leeway, but the Harp eventually put the result beyond doubt with a third goal ten minutes from time, before Our Boys grabbed a late consolation.

Harp's victory earned them an away tie against East End, who had reached the second round by default following the withdrawal of Dundee St. Andrew. Despite putting up a great fight, the PitkerroPark men bowed out of the Forfarshire Cup to the eventual winners of the competition following defeat by the odd-goal-in-seven.

In the aftermath of having been knocked out of the Forfarshire Cup by bitter rivals Harp, Our Boys were determined to avenge the defeat when the two sides met in their Scottish Cup tie, and prepared for the clash by making a couple of changes in the side for their friendly against Third Lanark at West Craigie on 26th September. Unfortunately, the changes did not work in their favour, and the Glasgow side ran out victors by nine-goals-to-two.

Undaunted, the team selection was changed again for the crunch Scottish Cup clash, and the team that took to the field at East Dock Street on Saturday 3rd October showed no fewer than six changes from that which had been knocked out of the county competition. As had been the case with the match played at the same venue a fortnight earlier, thousands of spectators made their way to the Harp ground, and a constant stream of horse-drawn buses and carriages could be seen making their way from the High Street towards East Dock Street in the hours leading up to kick-off.

In anticipation of a crowd similar to that which had paid to see the previous encounter, the Harp committee decided to open the gates a full three hours before the match was scheduled to start in order to avoid a crush, and by kick-off time there was close-on 9,000 spectators within the enclosure.

Although the crowd was smaller than that which had attended the previous match between the pair, a great atmosphere prevailed, and loud cheers greeted the teams as they made their way on to the park.

The game then started in a lively fashion, and both sides created chances amidst *"fast and furious play"*, but it was the Harp who eventually broke the deadlock after half-an-hour with a shot that went in off the post. During the second half, Harp stretched their lead to three goals, just as they had done in the previous meeting. The dark-blues eventually managed to pull a goal back, but any hopes of turning the tie around were dashed when the home side added a fourth, and Our Boys were out of the Scottish Cup.

This latest defeat to bitter rivals Harp was to have far-reaching consequences. In the weeks following the match, it slowly became apparent that there was general unrest within the Our Boys set-up, particularly amongst the players. Certain players were unhappy about how the team was being organised, in particular with regard to team selection, and by the end of October there was talk of the despondent players walking out on the club.

Matters came to a head when wholesale team changes were made for the home fixture against East End on 21st November 1885. With the rebels watching the action from the grandstand, a makeshift team of older players mixed with players promoted from the junior team pulled off a convincing 6-1 victory against their local rivals, and a message was sent loud and clear to the dissenters that Our Boys could function perfectly well without them!

Just a week later, a new team playing under the name of Wanderers, made up entirely from the rebel Our Boys players, challenged East End to a match at PitkerroPark and won by six goals without reply. Dundee not only had a new football club; it had a new club capable of competing with the best teams in the district!

Both East End and Our Boys then embarked on a series of challenge matches, and for their programme over the festive season both clubs arranged attractive fixtures. Just before Christmas, the dark-blues entertained Manchester side Greenheys, who were beaten by seven goals without reply, before both Cowlairs and Dumbarton attracted large crowds to WestCraigiePark at the beginning of January 1886.

Whilst Our Boys were playing Dumbarton, a short distance away at Pitkerro Park East End were engaged in a thrilling match against Clyde, where the visitors eventually won by five goals to four after the home side had held a 2-0 lead at the interval.

In February 1886, the feud between the dark-blues and their rebellious former players once again raised its ugly head when a match in aid of the local unemployed was arranged between Our Boys and Wanderers. In the days leading up to the encounter, the officials of both clubs became engaged in a public slagging match through the columns of the local press, and this bad feeling inevitably spilled on to the field of play on the day of the game.

During the first half, according to one press report, *"an incident thoroughly foreign to the game, and which threatened to result in something serious"* occurred, and play was halted for a few minutes. After order had been restored amongst the players and an unruly faction within the crowd of 4,000 spectators, play was allowed to continue. There were, however, further incidents as the game progressed, before the final whistle sounded with the score level at five goals apiece.

Our Boys pictured before the much-publicised fall-out that led to the formation of Wanderers F.C.

East End pictured with the Burns Charity Cup in 1900.

It has to be said that the condition of the WestCraigiePark playing surface, which was completely covered in frozen snow, contributed in no small way to these incidents. However, the Dundee Courier, on the following Monday morning, would not let the matter regarding unruly behaviour amongst the players and spectators rest, and included the following comments in their match report:

"Although there was no occasion for it, the play was unfortunately tainted to a more than warrantable extent, and in connection with this we would suggest to those who cannot take part in such an exciting game without letting their worst nature gain the ascendancy that they should seriously consider whether it would not be better for their own reputation and the reputation of the pastime and their club that they should content themselves with a position outside the ropes, where after a piece of good play they could use their hands in a perfectly legitimate manner".

Later that month, Our Boys had another chance to avenge their earlier defeats at the hands of Harp when the pair were drawn to face each other in the first round of the Burns Charity Cup. With heavy snow having fallen in the days leading up to the game, a gang of unemployed workmen repaid the goodwill recently shown them by the West Craigie club by clearing the park of snow on the eve of the match. Despite more heavy snow the following morning, the match went ahead in front of almost 6,000 spectators, but poor underfoot conditions coupled with a strong icy wind meant that good football was going to be impossible. When the referee's whistle eventually signalled the end of the game, it was the Harp who once again emerged victorious, this time by the rather convincing margin of seven-goals-to-two.

East End, who had been given a 'bye' in the first round of the charity competition, were drawn to face Harp at East Dock Street in the semi-final, where they were no match for the team that had by now established itself as the best in Dundee.

A one-sided first half saw the Harp run up a six-nil lead and, although it would appear that they slackened off a little during the second forty-five minutes, the home side went on to win by nine goals to one. Predictably, Harp went on to win the Burns Cup for the third year in succession after beating Strathmore 3-1 in the final.

East End were not too despondent at the end of season 1885/86, however, and in a speech made at their annual 'Festival and Assembly', club president Alexander Gow enthused about the progress that had been made over the past year. With a record of eleven victories from twenty-three matches played, along with three draws and nine defeats, he was of the opinion that the future looked very promising. The president was also full of enthusiasm for how the game of football had, in recent years, taken hold throughout Dundee; and stated that nearly every household in the Burgh had been smitten with 'football fever'!

Mr. Gow also emphasised the point that the East End Football Club had, in recent times, started to re-establish itself amongst Dundee's football elite by recruiting youthful players in favour of those who were perhaps past their best, stating that:

"The old broken-winded fossils had been drummed out – and the ranks filled with youths fired with enthusiasm and a genuine love of the game and who could play it when they liked with invincible determination".

Amidst thunderous applause, the president concluded by stating his opinion that by playing *"consistently and with spirit"*, the team would surely be rewarded with public support.

There was one other significant remark made during Mr. Gow's speech that is worth mentioning. At one point, he referred to the club as *"the wise men of the east"*, and in doing so he had inadvertently given them the nickname of 'The Wise Men'!

This moniker went on to become frequently used in match reports throughout the remainder of the club's history, and was generally regarded by all familiar with the game of football in Dundee as the official nickname of East End Football Club.

As for Our Boys, everyone associated with the club was also looking back on season 1885/86 in a positive manner, despite the well publicised fall out between the club and its players. At their annual festival, held in the Thistle Hall, club president Hunter stated his opinion that the results over the season had been *"very creditable"*, and was quick to point out that the team's performances before and after the exodus of players to the Wanderers had shown little change. Before the split, the team had played 16 matches of which 8 had been won, 7 lost, and one drawn. Since then, from 15 matches played, 7 had been won, 6 lost and 2 drawn. There were, however, several games still scheduled to be played before the curtain finally came down on the season.

Amidst thunderous applause, the president went on to say that the past year had been *"one of the most prosperous in the history of the club"*, and that the good reputation of Our Boys was spreading throughout the country, especially amongst those clubs that had journeyed through from the west in order to play challenge matches at West Craigie Park.

With such a positive attitude shown by those at the helm of both Our Boys and East End, the future of both clubs was now looking assured!

10

Contrasting Fortunes

Despite the positive atmosphere that had existed within the East End ranks at the end of the previous campaign, neither public support nor team spirit were very much in evidence when the new season got under way with a friendly against Broughty at Pitkerro Park on Saturday 4th September 1886.

In front of a *"meagre attendance"*, the wise-men went down by four-goals-to-one, with their play described as *"loose and slack"* by the local press. Two weeks later, the club suffered further humiliation when they were knocked out of the Forfarshire Cup at the first-round stage following a 5-1 thumping from Wanderers. The poor run of form continued and, at the end of September, in front of another meagre crowd at Pitkerro Park, East End went down in a challenge match to an under strength Strathmore side by five goals without reply.

In complete contrast, Our Boys kicked off the 1886/87 season in blistering style on 14th August when Hibernian were sent home to Edinburgh with their tails firmly between their legs following a 5-0 thumping at West Craigie. Further convincing friendly wins followed, including a nine-nil victory away to St. Johnstone and an impressive 4-1 home win over Glasgow Northern.

The 'Boys' were brought down to earth with a bump in mid-September, however, when Forfar Athletic triumphed 5-2 at West Craigie in a Scottish Cup tie to end the Dundee side's interest in the national competition at the first hurdle.

As for East End, the PitkerroPark side found themselves in round two without having kicked a ball after first round opponents Aberdeen withdrew from the competition.

Some dignity was restored to East End's recent form at the beginning of October, when Broughty were defeated by the odd-goal-in-nine in the second round of the tournament.

The wise-men were rewarded with a home tie against Dunblane in round three, and in front of a *"fair attendance of spectators"* at PitkerroPark on Saturday 23rd October, the honours were shared in an exciting tussle that ended all-square at three goals apiece.

The replay of the Scottish Cup tie was scheduled for the following Saturday, but unfortunately East End were faced with what turned out to be an insurmountable problem during the days leading up to the match.

In the late nineteenth century, Saturday mornings were part of the working week, which meant that it would be near-impossible for the players to finish work then travel through to Dunblane in time for kick-off unless they were granted permission to leave work early. When five of the club's key players were unable to obtain the necessary dispensation, East End felt that they had no other option but to withdraw from the competition. As the circumstances behind the withdrawal were, in the opinion of the committee, out-with the control of the club, the wise-men made an application to the Scottish Football Association for a refund of their ten shillings entry fee (50p in today's money). Not surprisingly, as the club had already participated in the first and second rounds, their appeal was rejected!

Our Boys had a more successful run than their near-neighbours in the county competition, and had kicked off their quest for the Forfarshire Cup with an exciting 6-5 victory over Broughty Ferry at West Craigie on 25th September.

The second round saw Friockheim, a village side, make the twenty mile trip south to Dundee, where they were well and truly thumped by twelve goals without reply.

Friockheim had actually been drawn at home, but opted to concede the advantage in return for a share of the gate money drawn from the *"considerable attendance"* that lined the ropes at WestCraigiePark.

The semi-final of the Forfarshire Cup paired Our Boys with Harp; and, as had also been the case in the three competitive meetings between the sides the previous season, great excitement prevailed in the days leading up to the game.

On Saturday 30th October, with an *"immense crowd"* inside Harp's East Dock Street ground, Our Boys started the game well, and soon had the Harp goal under pressure. Their superiority eventually paid off when they opened the scoring midway through the first half. The cup holders retaliated, however, and had turned the game around by half-time to lead 2-1.

Harp then took control of the match after the interval, and eventually ran out winners by five goals to two to knock the 'Boys' out of the county competition yet again. It was starting to look as if there was to be no way past their 'bogey team'!

Just a fortnight after their exit from the Forfarshire Cup, Our Boys were dealt another blow on Monday 15th November when their dressing room at West Craigie Park was broken into, and no fewer than fifty complete sets of kit, comprising jerseys, knickers and boots, were stolen.

The thieves also made off with a number of balls and other items, including an air pump for inflating the balls that was of great sentimental value, having been used by the club since its inception.

The break-in was witnessed by workmen at the adjacent Lilybank Foundry, who observed a number of men carrying sacks leaving the dressing room, which was located at the north end of WestCraigiePark, before making their exit through a hole in the fence.

With the value of the stolen items valued at around £60, a considerable sum of money in 1886, a huge impact had been made on the club's finances, and Our Boys were forced to cancel their trip to face Forfar Athletic on the following Saturday.

It would also appear that all was not well with East End as the year drew to a close. Following their exit from the Scottish Cup in late October, an air of despondency seemed to be affecting the club and its players.

Although Forfar Athletic had been defeated at StationPark in early November, things had started to go badly wrong on the field of play, and on 11th December they suffered a humiliating defeat by eleven goals to one against Strathmore at Rollo's Pier.

Remarkably, the wise-men had actually taken an early lead in this match, and at half-time the score was level at a goal apiece. In the second half, however, the home side scored ten times and, had it not been for the fact that three goals were disallowed, the final score could have been even worse!

A home clash with Harp, scheduled for Christmas Day, was then called off, with the club claiming that difficulties had arisen in connection with the match. With the club also having failed to arrange any matches over the New Year holiday period, it was becoming all too apparent that the difficulties spoken of were deep-rooted.

Things were looking up at WestCraigiePark, however, and after Our Boys had thumped Leith Harp 8-0 on Christmas Day, they made a rare trip west to face Port Glasgow Athletic on New Years Day 1887 at ClunePark, where they beat the home side 4-2.

Most of the talk in football circles during the festive period, however, was centred around Strathmore, who became the first Dundee club to venture south of the border.

On New Year's Day, a 2-0 victory was recorded against Lancashire side Hurst; then, two days later, the 'Strathie' lined up to face Aston Villa in Birmingham where, by all accounts, the players gave a good account of themselves, despite eventually going down by two-goals-to-one.

"The Scotchmen, though defeated, had certainly the worst of the luck, and deserved to win" commented the press, who went on to say that: *"The Villa had a splendid team, no fewer than nine of them being professionals"*.

The final match of the tour was played against Port Vale in Burslem on Tuesday 4th January, where the home side inflicted a 2-0 defeat.

On Saturday 8th January 1887, East End finally made a re-appearance when, according to the local press, they had *"whipped together a strong team"* to face Our Boys in a challenge match at West Craigie. Although the wise-men put up a good fight on the day, they eventually succumbed to the home side by three goals to one.

Both Our Boys and East End returned to competitive action in March when the 1886/87 Burns Charity Cup tournament got under way. At a meeting of the Forfarshire Association at the beginning of February, an application from Broughty to join the competition had been rejected, and it was agreed that once again only five teams would take part.

The draw was then made, and East End were handed a home tie against Strathmore at Pitkerro Park in the first round, with Our Boys, Harp and Wanderers given a 'bye' into the semi-final.

Before the first match was played, however, there was once again a degree of bickering, after it had been decreed at a meeting of the Forfarshire Association that: *"players who had played for one club in the county and Scottish ties could not play for another club in the Burns Cup"*.

This effectively ruled out the entire Strathmore team, and at a meeting of the Strathmore club on 21st February it was claimed that the rule *"was not only informal but illegal and contrary to common sense"*. Strathmore then protested to the F.F.A. about what they considered to be unfair discrimination, and pointed out that *"at least Wanderers, East End and Our Boys had broken this rule previously"*. When the Forfarshire Association refused to back down, Strathmore withdrew from the competition, and Lochee were invited to take their place.

The first round Burns Charity Cup tie between East End and Lochee eventually went ahead on Saturday 19th March at PitkerroPark, where the home side won a closely fought encounter 2-1 after scoring the winner in the final minute of the game.

They were rewarded with a semi-final against Wanderers, with Our Boys and Harp paired together yet again in the other half of the draw.

At West Craigie on Saturday 26th March, Our Boys hopes were high that they would finally be able to register a competitive victory over bitter rivals Harp. With the ground in pristine condition after having been levelled and rolled, the supporters looked forward to an exciting tussle, and just under 6,000 lined the ropes when the match got under way.

Playing up the slope during the first forty-five minutes, Our Boys weathered some early pressure from Harp before they opened the scoring amidst loud cheers mid-way through the first half. Despite both sides creating further chances, half-time arrived with Our Boys leading by that solitary goal.

With the slope in their favour during the second half, it looked very much like Our Boys' long standing bogey was about to be laid to rest, but Harp had other ideas. Following several missed chances by the dark-blues, the visitors equalised matters mid-way through the second period, and when the final whistle sounded the score was still level at a goal apiece.

A week later, the semi-final of the Burns Charity Cup between Our Boys and Harp was replayed at East Dock Street, where once again the same old story unfolded.

By half-time the home side were three goals ahead and, despite a determined struggle to reduce the leeway during the second forty-five minutes, Harp scored a fourth goal and Our Boys' Burns Cup campaign was over for another season.

On Saturday 9th April 1887, the second semi-final between East End and Wanderers went ahead at the latter's Morgan Park, which was situated on Mains Loan, in front of a crowd of 4,000. It turned out to be a day to forget for the wise-men, however, and a one-sided first half ended with the home side 5-0 ahead.

Any hopes of a second half revival by East End were wiped out as the Wanderers continued their onslaught on the visitors' goal unabated, and at the end of a grueling ninety minutes the Morgan Park side were declared victors by nine goals to one. It was a bitter pill for the wise-men to swallow.

A fortnight later, in front of a crowd of almost 9,000 at neutral WestCraigiePark, Wanderers ended Harp's hold on the Burns Charity Cup with a 4-1 victory.

Despite the fact that both Our Boys and East End had so far failed in their respective bids to reach the Forfarshire Cup Final, their second elevens achieved that very feat during season 1886/87. Following a 2-2 draw earlier in the season at Harp's EastDockStreetPark, Our Boys Rangers and East End Wanderers lined up at the same venue on the afternoon of

Thursday 14th April to contest the replayed final of the Second Eleven Forfarshire Cup. With the two sides level at two goals apiece during the second half, the Rangers stepped up a gear and scored four times to win the match by six-goals-to-two.

For the first time in their history Our Boys could claim to have silverware in their trophy cabinet!

As for the first team, Our Boys put their unsuccessful cup campaigns and their apparent inability to beat Harp in competitive matches behind them, and saw out the remainder of the season with a series of challenge games against varied opposition, including English side Elswick Rangers.

The curtain was finally brought down on the 'Boys' season with a 5-3 victory against a Motherwell and District Select at the beginning of June.

As for East End, it would appear that the players had little appetite for the game following their thumping from Wanderers and, a week later, several players were missing from the party when the team arrived fully an hour late in Blairgowrie for a match against the local side. It was no surprise when the Blairgowrie club won a rather one-sided game by five goals to one.

Under an air of despondency, the wise-men played out the remainder of their season with some uninspiring performances, and their 1886/87 campaign, in complete contrast to that of Our Boys, ended rather apathetically.

11

The Forfarshire Clubs Make their Mark

The air of despondency that had descended on PitkerroPark at the end of the previous campaign had all but disappeared when a promising start was made to season 1887/88. In the curtain raiser on Saturday 22nd August, the honours were shared in a respectable 1-1 draw with Harp at Pitkerro, before Broughty were soundly beaten 8-3 at the same venue a week later.

Over at West Craigie, Our Boys kicked off their season with a 3-0 victory over Staffordshire Cup holders Stoke-on-Trent, which was followed by defeats from both Wanderers and Strathmore before the month of August was rounded off with a 6-2 home win against their namesakes Blairgowrie Our Boys.

East End kicked off their competitive season on the first Saturday in September with a resounding victory away to Arbroath Strathmore in the first round of the Scottish Cup by an incredible thirteen-goals-to-one.

Reporting on the match, local newspaper The Arbroath Guide lamented that *"goal followed goal with disheartening frequency"*, before adding *"the goalkeeper had a peculiar fancy for letting his opponents have their own way"*. The newspaper did, however, conclude with the opinion that East End had been by far the superior side and that the result of the match had never been in doubt from the start.

In round two of the national competition, the wise-men journeyed north to face Kirriemuir side Lindertis on 24th September, only to be knocked out of the tournament in very controversial circumstances.

When the team arrived in Kirriemuir, they were dismayed to discover that the town's football pitch was just a stubble field, which had goalposts but no corner flags, and did not appear to have been marked off properly. An additional problem then manifested itself when the appointed referee failed to show up.

In order to have the game played, a 'neutral' was recruited from the crowd to take charge of the match. However, this 'unbiased' individual turned out to be a certain Mr. A. Gray, a resident of Kirriemuir who, it would appear, was an avid follower of his home town team!

The game kicked off as scheduled, and when Lindertis took the lead after just ten minutes, referee Gray could be heard cheering *"with might and main"*. By half-time, the home side were leading by three-goals-to one, leaving East End with a mountain to climb during the second half, especially as the Kirriemuir team appeared by all accounts to have an extra man in the form of the match official. The wise-men tried their best to right matters during the second period, but only managed to reduce the leeway by one goal, and the game ended with a 3-2 victory for Lindertis.

East End, however, were determined not to let the matter rest, and duly wrote to the Scottish Football Association to protest about both the referee and the state of the Kirriemuir pitch. At the monthly meeting of the S.F.A., held in Glasgow on 4th October 1887, the protest against Lindertis F.C. was heard.

The club's main protest, understandably, concerned the referee, Mr. Gray, who they had falsely been advised was 'neutral' and had no leanings towards either team. This, claimed the wise-men, could not have been further from the truth, as the gentleman in question had *"cheered and waved his hat in the air"* when the home side scored. He was also, they alleged, *"under the influence of liquor"*.

When the allegations were put to Mr. Gray, he denied profusely that he had been under the influence of alcohol, and claimed that the decisions he had made throughout the game had been *"fair and square"*. As to the charge that he had cheered and waved his hat when the home team scored, he replied that this could not possibly have been the case as he had *"worn no hat on the day in question"*.

Regarding the questions raised about the state of the pitch, Lindertis strenuously denied that their ground was a stubble field, and claimed that it had been correctly lined, although they did admit to having no corner flags. To East End's dismay, the protest was thrown out.

The club fared no better in the Forfarshire Cup. Following an impressive seven-nil home thrashing of Lochee in the first round on 10th September 1887, East End travelled north to face Forfar Athletic in round two of the county competition at Station Park, where by all accounts the team played well in a high-scoring encounter that ended in favour of the home side by six-goals-to-five.

Our Boys embarked on what was to be a highly successful Scottish Cup campaign with a 9-4 victory against Aberdeen at KittybrewsterPark at the beginning of September. Before the month was out, the dark-blues had recorded a 5-3 win over Montrose at WestCraigiePark in the second round, despite having gone two goals behind early in the match.

In round three, Our Boys were drawn to face Perth side Fair City Athletic at their BalhousiePark ground on 15th October, where five goals were scored without reply to book the dark-blues a place in the fourth round. When the draw was made, however, Our Boys were handed a 'bye', and with it a place in the last sixteen of the national competition.

The fifth round of the Scottish Cup saw Our Boys drawn to face Albion Rovers at home on 26th November 1887.

An advertisement for the Our Boys v Albion Rovers Scottish Cup tie in November 1887.

Great excitement preceded the match and, with the visitors having recorded a 14-0 score-line in a Lanarkshire Cup tie a week earlier, it was thought the home defence were going to have to be at their best to keep the Coatbridge side at bay.

The game, however, turned out to be something of a damp squib, and ended in controversial circumstances.

Near the end of the match, with Our Boys leading 3-1, Albion Rovers were refused a foul and, after remonstrating with the referee, decided to walk off the field. The dark-blues players then proceeded to casually walk the length of the pitch before calmly rolling the ball between the posts for goal number four. A subsequent protest by Albion Rovers on the grounds that the referee, Mr. Devlin of Dunfermline, was incompetent, was thrown out by the Scottish Football Associaton.

Our Boys had made it through to the last eight of the Scottish Cup, a stage of the competition that no team from north of the Firth of Tay had reached before, but they were not alone. Remarkably, adversaries Wanderers had also reached the quarter-finals, as had fellow Forfarshire rivals Arbroath!

To reach the last eight, Wanderers had disposed of Lochee, Aberdeen Rovers, Coupar Angus, Queen of the South Wanderers and Carfin Shamrock; whilst Arbroath had overcome Aberdeen side Orion, Dundee Strathmore, Oban, and Cowlairs.

With three Forfarshire sides in the draw, was there to be a mouth-watering local derby in order to fight it out for a place in the last four of the national competition?

Unfortunately, all three teams were kept apart, and all three were handed ties away from home. Our Boys faced a trip to Glasgow to face Cambuslang; Wanderers were drawn against Dunbartonshire side Renton, winners of the cup in 1885; and Arbroath's name came out of the hat to play Paisley side Abercorn.

On December 17th 1887, Our Boys lined up to face Cambuslang at their WhitefieldPark ground with a weakened side after two key players had called off. In front of a surprisingly sparse crowd of just over 1,000, the Dundee side started the game on the attack, but Cambuslang quickly gained control and by half-time were 2-0 ahead.

During the second forty-five minutes the play was all centred around Our Boys' goal, and unsurprisingly the home side added another four goals to their tally to win by six goals to nil. It was something of an anti-climax for the dark-blues, but the club had proved that they now had the ability to reach the latter stages of Scotland's premier football competition, which augured well for the future.

As for their fellow Forfarshire teams, Wanderers went down 5-1 to Renton, who went on to win the Scottish Cup for the second time when they beat Our Boys' conquerors Cambuslang in the final at Hampden Park. Arbroath, who had travelled through to Paisley by private rail coach, were beaten 3-1 by Abercorn.

Paling into the background somewhat during Our Boys' Scottish Cup run was their 1887/88 Forfarshire Cup campaign. In the first round, Kirriemuir side Lindertis made the journey south to WestCraigiePark, and were soundly beaten 8-1. In the second round, however, Our Boys were thumped by an embarrassing twelve-goals-to-nil at the same venue on 1st October by Arbroath, who went on to win the county cup the following month by the almost equally convincing score-line of 10-2 against Strathmore in the final at East Dock Street.

East End, meantime, were still suffering apathy within the ranks. For their match against Fair City Athletic in Perth on 19th November, two players failed to show up, and club president William McLean was forced to don the centre-half jersey.

With no other member of the East End party even remotely fit enough to endure ninety-minutes on a football field, the club had no other option but to fill the other vacant place in the side by fielding one of the Perth club's third eleven. Surprisingly, the visitors still managed to win convincingly by four-goals-to-one!

Apart from that result, however, victories had been few and far between for the wise-men following their exit from both the Scottish Cup and the Forfarshire Cup. In addition, the club's plight was not helped when illness spread through the team in late December, forcing the cancellation of matches that had been scheduled to be played over the festive period.

On Saturday 7th January 1888, East End returned to action against Strathmore at Rollo's Pier, where a last-minute equaliser earned them a share of the honours in a thrilling 5-5 draw. It would appear that the fortunes of the club were now about to turn the corner, prompting one press reporter to comment: *"The Wise Men have at present a better eleven than they are generally given credit for"*.

This opinion was vindicated over the following two Saturdays, when Our Boys were held to a 1-1 draw at Pitkerro Park before Broughty were convincingly beaten by four goals to one at the same venue.

Our Boys, meanwhile, had participated in a full programme over the New Year holiday period, with home challenge matches played out against Mossend Swifts and Airdrieonians followed up by a visit from Dunfermline Athletic. A proposed meeting with Arthurlie on 2nd January was postponed due to the WestCraigiePark playing surface being declared *"hard as flint"*.

On Saturday 18th February, Our Boys Rangers, the club's second eleven, once again achieved what the first team could not, when they won the Second Eleven Forfarshire Cup for the second year in a row.

With a crowd of several thousand looking on at the neutral venue of Rollo's Pier, the Our Boys' second string scored the winning goal in the closing minutes to defeat their Harp counterparts by the odd-goal-in-seven, with the loud cheers of their supporters ringing in their ears.

The Burns Charity Cup, the winners of which were now widely accepted as being Champions of Dundee, once again presented the opportunity for both Our Boys and East End to win silverware before the end of the season.

It was the latter club who were first to engage in the competition when they took on Strathmore in a first round tie at Rollo's Pier on 3rd March 1888, but it turned out that this match was certainly not one for the purists.

Strathmore were by far the better side during the opening forty-five minutes, but despite having the East End goal under severe pressure, the teams retired at half-time all-square at a goal apiece. During the second half, it was more of the same from the home side, but when the final whistle blew the score was level at 3-3.

It would appear, from all accounts, that the wise-men had avoided defeat by sheer physical force rather than by football skills, with centre-half Knowles in particular coming in for criticism for the way he had manhandled Strathmore's centre-forward Dickson throughout the game.

In summing up the action, the Dundee Courier commented on the Monday following the match:

"As an exhibition of football the game was almost an utter failure, and if a living embodiment of charity could have witnessed it she

would have wept to see done in her name such things as abounded in the contest. Several of the men, evidently labouring under great excitement "went for their opponents, to the total disregard of the ball", and those who desired to play the game found it, as a rule, quite impossible to do so".

"The attention of Knowles to Dickson formed an outstanding feature of the fight, the former acting throughout as if he were the shadow of the latter, who was also at times held by the neck and arms, and on two or three occasions was tripped up".

The replay was scheduled for PitkerroPark on the following Saturday afternoon, and on the eve of the match the Evening Telegraph felt compelled to comment:

"Last week's drawn game gave rise to a great deal of unnecessary roughness, but it hoped that tomorrow a change for the better will take place. At any rate the public will look for a purer exhibition of the game, and will not fail to see where the fault lies".

"Let "Play the ball, not the man," be the motto of each side this time, and the spectators will see something that will encourage them to further patronise the Charity ties, instead of turning them away".

In front of a large crowd at Pitkerro Park, the wise-men heeded the advice, and let football skills rather than rough play dictate the run of the game. Playing down the slope during the first half, they built up a commanding 4-1 interval lead, and following an evenly-contested second forty-five minutes, East End booked their place in the semi-final of the Burns Cup with a 5-2 victory.

In the last four of the competition, East End were drawn at home to Wanderers, who had knocked out tournament favourites Harp in the previous round by the convincing score of 5-1. Despite a strong wind blowing up Pitkerro Park, the ground was in perfect condition for the semi-final, and a large crowd lined the ropes in anticipation of a good game of football. Not one of the spectators, however, could have predicted how the match they were about to witness would turn out.

Playing downhill from the start, it looked very much like East End were going to make full use of the slope during the first half, and the Wanderers goal led a charmed life during the opening exchanges.

After the crossbar had come to the visitors' rescue, it was no surprise when the wise-men eventually broke the deadlock after only five minutes' play. From that point of the game onwards, however, the luck was all with the Wanderers.

Although the home side managed to create further chances, and were unfortunate to have a goal disallowed for off-side, the visitors scored an incredible five times before the interval to build up a commanding lead. During the second forty-five minutes, with the incline in their favour, Wanderers registered a further three goals to run out convincing 8-1 winners.

In the other semi-final, Our Boys and Lochee, who had both received a 'bye' in the first round, lined up to face each other at West Craigie Park. Beautiful weather and a vociferous crowd greeted the teams as they emerged from the dressing rooms, and a fast and exciting game then commenced. Lochee were the first to draw blood after ten minutes' play, but this only served to sting the dark-blues into action, and when the half-time whistle sounded the ground team were 2-1 ahead.

The second half had only just started when Our Boys increased their tally to three, and although the visitors pulled a goal back, the dark-blues added another couple of counters late in the game to put the result beyond doubt. At the end of an entertaining match, Our Boys were declared winners by five-goals-to-two, and were through to the Burns Charity Cup Final.

The eagerly anticipated final of the tournament went ahead at East Dock Street on Saturday 12th May 1888, and for fully an hour before the advertised kick-off time the streets surrounding the ground were *"thronged with an eager crowd of enthusiastic followers of the competing clubs"*. As the supporters formed long queues at the pay booths, some loud-mouthed advocates of the Wanderers were heard to proclaim that they anticipated a double-figure tally of goals for their favourites, and that Our Boys would fail to register a single goal.

Devotees of the dark-blues gave as good as they got, however, and the good-natured banter continued once both sets of supporters were inside the ground, as the atmosphere built with kick-off fast approaching. It seemed that the bad feeling that had once existed between the clubs, in the wake of their much-publicised split over two years earlier, was now largely forgotten. On the terraces at least!

Both teams entered the field to rousing cheers, and when play eventually got under way there was little to choose between the sides. After half-an-hour, however, Wanderers broke the deadlock, and before half-time the Morgan Park men had doubled their tally.

Our Boys started the second period in determined fashion, and almost scored straight from the kick-off, but the ball whistled just over the cross-bar. The pressure on the Wanderers goal was maintained, and the dark-blues eventually succeeded in registering a goal amidst loud cheering with about ten minutes of the second half gone. Our Boys were now in complete control of the match, and the Wanderers had their goalkeeper to thank for preserving their slender lead as the second half progressed.

Twenty-five minutes into the second period, however, the Wanderers scored a third goal against the run of play, before quickly adding a fourth to put the outcome beyond reasonable doubt. Our Boys refused to give up, and again managed to beat the Wanderers custodian, but it was all too late and

Wanderers ran out winners by four-goals-to-two to lift the Burns Charity Cup for the second year in a row.

All things considered, however, it had been a good season for Our Boys. Some notable victories had been recorded, and some embarrassing defeats had been suffered, but with Our Boys Rangers having won the Second Eleven Cup for a second time, the future of the club looked to be secure on the playing side.

As for the wise-men, the club remained upbeat despite some heavy defeats throughout the 1887/88 campaign, and despite the apparent apathy shown by certain players. East End's second eleven had also had a good season and, like Our Boys, the club could look forward to their reserve players eventually making their mark in the first team.

12

More Battles and More Bickering

East End kicked off season 1888/89 by testing their strength against Burntisland Thistle, one of the more prominent Fife clubs at that time, in front of a *"fair turnout of spectators"* at PitkerroPark on 25th August. Victory by six-goals-to-two was the outcome, and victory by such a margin against a club of the calibre of Burntisland must surely have instilled confidence for the forthcoming campaign. Our Boys, on the other hand, lost 5-2 in their opening game against Wanderers, which was followed up with a 4-2 defeat at the hands of Harp.

The draw for the first round of the Scottish Cup then paired Our Boys with East End, and the match was scheduled to be played on Saturday 1st September 1888 at West Craigie. If early season form was anything to go by, then the wise-men reckoned they were in with a chance of progressing to round two at the expense of their near-neighbours!

Despite wet weather conditions, a large crowd turned out for the cup-tie, and were treated to a thrilling display by both sides. Unfortunately, their enjoyment was marred by ugly scenes late in the game. An evenly-contested first half had ended all-square at a goal apiece, and shortly after half-time both sides had registered another goal. Three goals in quick succession for the home team, however, put Our Boys in control, with the score standing at 5-2. It was at this point that all-hell broke loose.

Fraying tempers had been getting the better of certain players as the match progressed, and fierce fighting broke out between the two teams shortly after the fifth goal had been registered.

Two of the home players were subsequently forced to retire with injuries sustained in the battle; but, as they were making their way towards the dressing room, another fight broke out between another two players, who set about each other in the centre of the field. The scene is perhaps best described by the report which appeared in the following Monday's edition of the Dundee Courier:

"Two of the players were engaged in a regular prize-fighting exhibition, inflicting and averting blows in a manner which would have done credit to professional pugilists. The combatants closed and rolled over, pounding away at each other with great vigour. They were, however, ultimately separated, and the teams engaged in a wordy wrangle in midfield, a number of them gesticulating wildly.

When the match was eventually re-started, East End scored twice to reduce the leeway, but the home side held on until the final whistle to win the match by five-goals-to-four.

The following round of the Scottish Cup saw Our Boys paired with Lochee, who were defeated 5-2 at West Craigie despite the home side having to play almost the entire second half with ten men after left-back Robertson had been forced to retire through injury.

In round three, Our Boys were drawn to face Harp, again at WestCraigiePark. With their old foes now just a shadow of the team they had once been, it was widely anticipated that the dark-blues would finally be able to put their bogey to rest and claim a competitive victory over the 'Irishmen'. Their supporters were not disappointed, as Our Boys won a place in round four of the Scottish Cup following a 2-1 victory, which by all accounts did not reflect the home side's superiority throughout the game.

In round four, the 'Boys' were handed a trip west to face Abercorn, who had reached the semi-finals of the national competition the previous season.

The Paisley side were, at the time, in great goal-scoring form, having disposed of Thornliebank by eight-goals-to-nil in the previous round. The dark-blues defence was going to have to be at its very best to avoid conceding a 'barrowload'.

One local press reporter, on the eve of the cup-tie, came up with a novel and rather tongue-in-cheek suggestion to keep the score respectable. The columnist had observed that Abercorn's Blackstoun Park lay adjacent to a gas works and, in the unlikely event that Our Boys found themselves a goal ahead, he proposed that the ball be kicked over the wall, concluding: *"Everyone will admit that to search for a ball in a gas work is not easy matter"*.

Unfortunately, when the match was played on 3rd November 1888, Our Boys never had the opportunity to put the cunning plan into operation. Eleven goals had been conceded before the home 'keeper was finally beaten to register a late consolation goal for the Dundee side!

Our Boys quest for the Forfarshire Cup in season 1888/89 was a disappointing one. Having received a 'bye' in the first round, the club's first match in the competition came a fortnight after their Scottish Cup exit in the form of a second round clash with Arbroath at Gayfield, where the home side progressed to the semi-final with a 4-2 victory.

Just a week later, however, the dark-blues recorded a much-needed confidence boost with an incredible 11-3 home victory over Forfar Athletic; who had, just a week earlier, beaten Wanderers in a Forfarshire Cup tie. Perhaps matters at West Craigie weren't so bad after all!

For East End, the Forfarshire Cup campaign that season turned out to be their best yet. Drawn to face Harp at East Dock Street in the first round, East End did themselves proud with a 3-2 victory to earn a second-round clash with Montrose.

With the 'Gable-Endies' having thrashed East End 6-3 in a friendly at Links Park just a fortnight earlier, a large crowd turned out for the match, played at Pitkerro Park on Saturday 17th November 1888, to see if the wise-men could avenge the heavy defeat.

They were not to be disappointed. Despite losing 2-1 at half-time, East End turned up the heat in the second-half, and eventually won the tie by seven-goals-to-three.

The wise-men were rewarded for their efforts with a home semi-final clash against Forfar Athletic on 15th December, and once again a large crowd lined the ropes at PitkerroPark. In perfect conditions for football, East End got the match under way, but the visitors quickly gained control and took an early lead. The wise-men came back strongly, however, and rattled in an incredible five goals in quick succession amidst the deafening cheers of the home supporters.

Try as they might during the second half, Forfar Athletic couldn't redeem themselves from their first-half drubbing and, when the final whistle sounded, it was the jubilant East End players and supporters who were celebrating, having managed to reach the final of the Forfarshire Cup for the first time in their history with a 6-3 victory!

The final of the county competition, billed as *"one of the hottest contests that has ever taken place"*, was played on Saturday 12th January 1889 in front of a crowd of several thousand at Harp's East Dock Street ground. Fully half-an-hour before kick-off, the crowd was standing several rows deep around the ropes, whilst the grandstand was reported to be almost full.

In a match described as *"par excellence"* by the local press, the crowd was treated to a thrilling encounter in which East End had their chances to score early in the game. However, when the half-time whistle sounded, it was the 'Red-Lichties' who held the upper hand with a single goal lead.

In the second half, Arbroath eventually managed to double their advantage, leaving the wise-men with a mountain to climb if they were to have any chance of landing the trophy for the first time. Hopes were raised when a goal was eventually pulled back, but although the team *"worked like very demons"* during the closing stages, East End failed to find the equaliser despite creating several chances. When the final whistle sounded, it was Arbroath who were declared victors by two-goals-to-one.

With involvement in the national and county cup competitions now over, and with the Burns Cup competition still several weeks away, East End and Our Boys filled their fixture lists with a series of challenge matches during the early weeks of 1889. Players from both clubs were also selected to play for the Forfarshire team scheduled to play Lanarkshire in the inter-county match at Airdrie in February.

The most notable challenge match played by either side at this time was the visit of Third Lanark to play Our Boys at West Craigie on 23rd February. The Glasgow side, who had won the Scottish Cup by beating Celtic at Hampden just a few weeks earlier, fielded all but three of their cup winning side, and won convincingly by seven-goals-to-three in front of 4,000 spectators.

One local club, however, decided to venture further afield in their quest for challenge matches. Just over two years after their previous visit to England, Strathmore made a second trip south of the border during the early weeks of 1889 and, in front of a crowd of 6,000 on Saturday 16th February, they faced Everton at their then home of Anfield, the future home of Liverpool Football Club.

The Dundee side *"received a hearty reception"* according to the Lancashire Saturday evening newspaper 'Football Field', and when the match got under way, the visitors stunned Everton by taking an early lead.

The home side, however, playing with the wind at their backs during the second half, eventually showed their superiority and ran out 5-1 winners. Incidentally, one of the very first programmes ever produced for a football match was issued for this game!

Before returning to Dundee, a tired and weary Strathmore met old adversaries Preston North End at Deepdale, where, *"ankle deep in mud"* they succumbed to the Lancashire side by a humiliating fifteen-goals-to-one.

The Burns Charity Cup for season 1888/89 eventually got under way at the end of March and, with Dundee having been granted city status earlier in the year, the local clubs now had the added incentive of being crowned the first champions of the City of Dundee!

In the draw for the first round, Our Boys were given another chance to record a first-ever Burns Cup victory over bogey team Harp; whilst East End were drawn to face Strathmore.

The first tie to be played was Harp v Our Boys at East Dock Street on 23rd March, where a crowd of over 4,000 assembled in weather that was *"everything that could be desired"* to witness the action. After an evenly contested opening period, it was the dark-blues who drew first blood, but Harp came back strongly and equalised mid-way through the first half. Our Boys then stepped up their game, and when the half-time whistle sounded they were 2-1 ahead.

When the second half got under way, it looked very much like the home side were about to level matters, but Our Boys weathered the storm and eventually went 3-1 ahead through a disputed header that Harp claimed had never crossed the line.

Despite end-to-end play during the remainder of the match, there was no further scoring, and when the final whistle sounded the Our Boys' players and supporters celebrated a long-awaited victory over Harp in the Burns Charity Cup.

Their celebrations, however, turned out to be short lived. Following the match, Harp lodged no fewer than four protests; firstly, that Our Boys' outside-left, Duncan, was ineligible as he had turned out for other clubs in cup-ties that season; secondly, the aforementioned player was not a club member of Our Boys; thirdly, that the same player was not registered to play for Our Boys; and finally, that the second and third goals scored by Our Boys were *"illegal"*.

At a subsequent meeting of the Forfarshire Football Association, held during the following midweek, the complaint made by Harp on the grounds that an ineligible player had been fielded was upheld. Consequently, Our Boys were thrown out of the competition, despite an offer from Harp to replay the tie, and the 'Irishmen' progressed to the semi-final.

East End's Charity Cup campaign got under way at PitkerroPark on 6th April. With the final whistle about to sound at the end of an exciting cup-tie, and with East End leading 4-3, the wise-men thought they were about to progress in the competition at the expense of Strathmore. The visitors had other ideas, however, and with virtually the last kick of the ball scored the equaliser, which *"produced a wild shout of elation from all over the field"*.

The replay went ahead at Rollo's Pier a week later, where Strathmore, playing with a strong gale-force wind at their backs, ran up a 3-0 lead inside the first fifteen minutes. When half-time was called, the home side held a commanding 4-1 lead; and, just minutes into the second period, scored a fifth. The wise-men refused to give up, however, and using the wind to their advantage managed to reduce the leeway to just one goal with twenty minutes of the match remaining. Despite intense pressure from East End on the Strathmore goal as the minutes ticked away, the home side broke away in the dying seconds to put the tie beyond doubt with goal number six.

There could be no doubt that the Burns Charity Cup, now in its sixth season, was a prestigious tournament, and one which was looked forward to with relish. The competition regularly produced exciting tussles, and huge crowds were attracted to the charity cup ties. However, a huge row regarding how the gate money was distributed was about to break out.

The eventual finalists of the Burns Charity Cup in season 1888/89 were Harp and Wanderers, who had faced each other in front of almost 5,000 spectators at WestCraigiePark on Saturday 11th May. Record drawings for the charity competition of £68-17 had been realised, and after the match, which finished all-square at 2-2, representatives of both sides made a request to the Forfarshire Football Association for both Harp and Wanderers to receive a share of the takings from the replay, as they were *"sorely in need of funds"*.

The F.F.A. refused, and decreed that the replay was to go ahead on Wednesday 15th May at neutral West Craigie, with all profits raised once again going directly to the Burns Association. Both clubs refused to take part in the match.

Instead, Harp and Wanderers made arrangements for an 'unofficial' Burns Cup Final replay, to take place at East Dock Street on the following Saturday, where Wanderers won by three goals to nil. The entire proceeds of this match, which was witnessed by just over 2,000 spectators, was split between the two clubs.

Incensed by the rebellious attitude shown by Harp and Wanderers, the Forfarshire Football Association consequently decided to wash its hands of all future involvement in the Burns Charity Cup. At the A.G.M. of the Association, held at the end of May 1889, it was recommended that in future the charity competition be governed by representatives from the Burns Association along with delegates from each of the participating clubs.

Our Boys played out the remaining weeks of the 1888/89 season by stamping their authority on the local football scene. On the Saturday following their Burns Cup exit, Arbroath were put to the sword at West Craigie by seven-goals-to-one, before Montrose were defeated 2-1 at LinksPark.

An eight-nil victory away to St. Johnstone then followed, before Wanderers were overcome 9-3 in the Boys' next home appearance at the end of April. There then followed a remarkable 13-2 thumping of Strathmore at West Craigie on 4th May. The season was rounded off with an 8-2 success against East End at PitkerroPark, to record the dark-blues twenty-first victory of the season from thirty-four games played.

The growing popularity of the game in Dundee, and the large crowds that were now turning up at WestCraigiePark, was now starting to cause problems for the local public transport system. The football ground was at this time served by a small horse-drawn tram which terminated at the south-west corner of BaxterPark, from where the entrance to WestCraigiePark was an easy two-minute walk. With the ground being used not only for Our Boys' home games, but as a neutral venue for cup ties, this service was proving to be woefully inadequate.

Letters were sent to the local newspapers complaining about the service, demanding that the previously used steam trams be re-instated. It was now simply impossible to board the horse-drawn tram on match days, forcing hundreds of supporters to use an alternative steam tram service as far as the VictoriaBridge, at the junction of Victoria Road and Victoria Street. From here, football followers were faced with a walk of half-a-mile to WestCraigiePark.

Visitors to East End's PitkerroPark, on the other hand, had no such problem with having to walk any distance, as they were able to take the steam trams as far as the MorganHospital terminus, which was within easy reach of the ground.

The Dundee and District Tramway Company's horse-drawn and steam vehicles of the type that would have been used to transport football supporters from the centre of Dundee to both WestCraigiePark and PitkerroPark on match days.

That said, the more spacious steam trams that ran frequently from the city centre to both VictoriaBridge and MorganHospital were still filled to overflowing on match days, with around sixty passengers crammed into each car. Passengers not bound for the football complained bitterly that they were being forced to take earlier or later trams if they wished to enjoy a seat!

East End also proved that they were still a side to be reckoned with as the 1888/89 season drew to a close, with some impressive victories recorded over the county's top teams. Just a fortnight after their Burns Cup exit, the wise-men gained revenge over Arbroath, their conquerors in the Forfarshire Cup final, in front of a big crowd at Gayfield. Losing 2-1 at half-time, East End eventually ran out 5-4 winners in an exciting match which saw the lead change hands three times during the second half.

The wise-men rounded off their campaign in impressive form, save for the aforementioned 8-2 drubbing at the hands of Our Boys, with a 3-1 victory over Harp at Pitkerro Park, followed up with a 7-1 hammering of Wanderers at the same venue.

Before the curtain finally came down on the season, both Our Boys and East End were represented in a match between Forfarshire and an All-Scotland Eleven, which was played at Harp's East Dock Street ground on Saturday 25th May.

The Forfarshire select side, which included players from both Our Boys and East End, had won all four matches played that season; against Ayrshire, Stirlingshire, Lanarkshire and Perthshire. The county team now had a golden opportunity to test themselves against a side containing players drawn from the country's top clubs.

Appearing in the All-Scotland team were players from Rangers, Partick Thistle, Clyde, St. Mirren, Cowlairs,

Battlefield, Abercorn and Cambuslang; the majority of whom were Scottish internationalists.

On a swelteringly hot afternoon, in front of a huge crowd, an entertaining match ended 3-1 in favour of the home side. It was a result that sent a message loud and clear that the brand of football played north of the Tay was improving rapidly, and that the Dundee sides would, before long, be able to compete with the best in the land!

13

The Re-emergence of East End

East End finally made their mark on the country's premier tournament, the Scottish Cup, during season 1889/90, when they managed to reach the quarter-finals of the competition.

The first round, on 7th September, saw the wise-men handed an away tie against Broughty which, despite some very rough play by the home side, was successfully negotiated thanks to a 6-1 victory.

The second round paired East End with Wanderers, and the match went ahead at Wanderers' Morgan Park on Saturday 28th September 1889 in front of *"a good turn out of spectators"*, who were treated to a rather one-sided display by the wise-men. The visitors eventually won 2-0, but by all accounts they would have won by a much larger score-line had their passing not been hampered by *"a strong north-easterly gale"*.

In round three, East End were drawn away from home yet again, but this time only as far as neighbours Our Boys. A crowd of over 4,000 lined the ropes at WestCraigiePark on 19th October, where both teams struggled to keep their feet on the wet and slippery surface. As an evenly contested first-half was drawing to a close, the wise-men drew first blood, and retired for their half-time cup of tea with a one-goal advantage.

The second period turned out to be a ding-dong affair, with both sides scoring twice. Despite a late onslaught by Our Boys, East End held out to win by the odd-goal-in-five, and were rewarded for their efforts with a fourth round home clash with the formidable Glasgow side Cambuslang, holders of the Glasgow Cup.

With PitkerroPark deemed unsuitable to host such a prestigious cup-tie, the match was moved to Harp's East Dock Street ground, where a crowd of almost 5,000 paid to see the action on Saturday 9th November 1889.

Following an evenly-contested first half, during which four goals were shared, both sides desperately fought to gain the advantage during a fiercely contested second period. Then, just when it looked like a replay would be required to decide the tie, team captain Longair scored a late winner for the wisemen amidst *"great cheering and waving of hats and handkerchiefs"*.

Far from accepting defeat in a sportsman-like manner, however, Cambuslang decided to protest to the Scottish Football Association on *"several grounds"* regarding the manner in which they had been knocked out of the cup. The main reasons for their protest were that the match had been officiated by a local man after the appointed referee had failed to turn up, and that the game had started late, causing the latter stages to be played out in near-darkness, at which point the winning goal had been scored. The protest was upheld, and the S.F.A. decreed that the tie be replayed.

On Saturday 23rd November, East End and Cambuslang lined up for a second time to decide their fourth round Scottish Cup tie, this time at Strathmore's Rollo's Pier, in front of a crowd which again numbered around 5,000. When the Glasgow side took to the field five minutes before the advertised kick-off, they were greeted by *"a good hearty groan"* from the crowd, which was, according to the local press, *"indicative only of the great dissatisfaction felt in this quarter with the decision of the Association"*.

East End, determined to prove that they had been worthy winners in the previous match at East Dock Street, controlled the first half and, when the interval arrived, they were three goals to the good.

It has to be said, however, that in winning the toss to determine which way the teams should play during the first forty-five minutes, the wise-men had elected to play with a strong sun at their backs.

This proved to be a distinct advantage as the game progressed, as by the time the second half got under way, the sun had all but disappeared. The remainder of the match was played out with no team disadvantaged by the strong rays.

The home supporters were, at the start of the second half, certain that victory was theirs, but the visitors then stepped up their game, and eventually pulled a goal back on the hour-mark. Then, with ten minutes left on the clock, poor defending resulted in Cambuslang adding a second. However, despite some late pressure from the 'strangers', the wise-men held out to win once again by the odd-goal-in-five.

Just a week later, East End made the long journey south to the Scottish borders to face Moffat in the fifth round of the competition. The home side, described in the press as being a *"crack team"*, attacked from the start, and stunned the wise-men with two goals inside the first five minutes.

East End desperately tried to get back into the game, but struggled with the heavy underfoot conditions, and when the interval arrived the home side were still leading by two-goals-to-nil.

It would appear that the half-time team talk did the visitors a power of good, and they pulled a goal back within minutes of the re-start.

East End continued to press, and eventually their superiority paid off when a Moffat defender put the ball in his own net following some intense pressure from the wise-men. Despite a late onslaught from the home side, the final whistle eventually sounded with the score all-square at two goals apiece.

On the following Saturday, 7th December 1889, East End and Moffat lined up to face each other at Harp's East Dock Street to decide their Scottish Cup tie, where a crowd of well over 5,000 assembled in weather described as *"being of the finest possible character for the game"*.

The match got under way in blistering fashion, and inside a quarter-of-an-hour both sides had managed to register a goal. It was East End who were the more determined side, however, and by half-time they had scored two more goals, *"to the enthusiastically-expressed delight of the spectators"*, to lead 3-1. Despite re-arranging their team at the start of the second half, Moffat could do nothing to thwart the determination of the East End forwards, and when the final whistle sounded the score stood at 5-1 in favour of the wise-men.

East End were through to the quarter-final of the Scottish Cup, but were then faced with the formidable task of having to overcome one of the country's top clubs, Vale of Leven. This famous old club, who hailed from the West Dunbartonshire town of Alexandria, had the distinction of having won the Scottish Cup no fewer than three times during the 1870's.

In order to give the team the best possible preparations for their quarter-final tie, the players and club officials made their way through to Glasgow on Friday 20th December, where they stayed overnight in a hotel before proceeding further west to Alexandria the following morning.

On a bright and sunny Saturday afternoon, with conditions perfect for football, East End and Vale of Leven lined up for the match that would decide which one of the two teams would make it through to the last four of the Scottish Cup. As expected, the Dundee side found the going tough against their more experienced opponents and, despite holding out for half-an-hour, found themselves two goals behind at the interval.

The wise-men, who were unaccustomed to playing on such a long and wide park, had also been weakened during the first half when half-back Spalding had picked up an injury. The player bravely battled on, but when the team was further weakened by an injury to forward Longair, who was forced to retire with a twisted leg, there was no way back for East End, who eventually went down by four goals without reply.

For the record, Vale of Leven went on to reach the Scottish Cup Final that season, where they lost to Queen's Park.

As for Our Boys, the WestCraigiePark side's prospects for the season were looking good after Glasgow Thistle, a highly respected side, had been soundly beaten in the club's opening fixture, which was followed up with a resounding 6-1 victory away to Forfar Athletic.

The dark-blues were drawn to face Strathmore at home in the first round of the Scottish Cup on Saturday 7th September; a fixture they were expected to win, with the Dundee Courier commenting on the eve of the match:

"Our Boysnever were in a stronger condition, and the heavy defeats which they have inflicted on such crack teams as the Glasgow Thistle and the Forfar Athletic this season already have buoyed their supporters up to conclude that they will gain an easy victory".

Their supporters were not to be disappointed. With the weather perfect for the occasion, and with the West Craigie playing surface *"in capital order"*, a 6-3 victory was recorded to knock the 'Strathie' out of the competition and see Our Boys safely through to the second round.

The dark-blues were rewarded with a clash against old foes Harp at East Dock Street on Saturday 28th September, where an incredible match ensued. After the home side had scored four times to lead 4-1 at half-time, it looked very much like Our Boys' old bogey had reared its ugly head once again.

With the wind at their backs during the second half, however, the Boys scored three times within ten minutes of the restart to equalise matters, before going on to command a 6-4 lead. Harp tried desperately to come back into the game, but only managed to reduce the deficit by one goal and, when the final whistle sounded at the end of a fast and exciting match, Our Boys were declared winners by six-goals-to-five.

However, that's as far as the dark-blues managed to progress in the 1889/90 Scottish Cup, with East End, as stated previously, managing to overcome the West Craigie Park side in round three.

After bowing out of the Scottish Cup, Our Boys turned their attention to the Forfarshire Cup, and when the names came out of the hat for the first round the dark-blues were drawn to face old adversaries Wanderers at WestCraigiePark on 26th October, just a week after their Scottish Cup exit.

In front of a large crowd, and with underfoot conditions slippery due to the inclement weather, the dark-blues booked their place in the second round of the Forfarshire Cup with a 6-2 victory. When the final whistle sounded, however, one of the Wanderers' men, McMahon, decided to vent his frustration on Linton, of Our Boys, and threw a punch, after which a fully-blown fist fight ensued.

The two combatants were immediately surrounded by a crowd of supporters from both sides, and two of that number then decided to exchange blows. As soon as these fights had been broken up by the more law-abiding spectators, however, more fights broke out on other parts of the field!

At a subsequent meeting of the Forfarshire Football Association, a complaint against McMahon for threatening and assaulting Linton was heard, and the Wanderers' player was suspended for a month.

The two sides had been scheduled to meet again on the following Saturday in a friendly at Wanderers' Morgan Park, but fearing that further trouble might break out similar to that ignominious encounter at West Craigie, Our Boys decided to pull out of the match.

This decision incensed the Wanderers secretary, as it left his club with a blank Saturday, and the club official felt compelled to vent his feelings via the local press. The Wanderers secretary was also adamant that his player had been a victim of the incident at WestCraigiePark rather than the perpetrator, stating:

"The Boys have justified their name by a very childish action, viz., refusing to play off their fixture with us on Morgan Park tomorrow. They are frightened that something should happen, so they say, and they refuse to play us for a month yet. I ask fairly and squarely did ever anything done by us on any former occasion, by us I mean both our team and their supporters, frighten the Craigie men? Nothing, unless it be the recollection of former defeats, and the prospect of their being repeated. The Forfarshire Association have seen fit in their wisdom to suspend J. McMahon for a month, and on what grounds? Is it because an Our Boys player used filthy language towards him? Is it because said player sneakingly assaulted him on the field? Or is it because McMahon, keeping himself cool until the match finished, then attempted to retaliate? These are questions which every Wanderer, aye, every independent spectator, wishes answered".

The secretary of Our Boys was not slow to respond, and vehemently rebuffed the accusation that his player had been in any way to blame:

"Referring to the cancelling of our fixture with the Wanderers, the following were our reasons for doing so, viz. : — That we were justified in doing so in the interests of football, as a few scenes similar to the one that happened at West Craigie last Saturday are likely to disgust the respectable portion of the football public, and bring football generally into disrepute".

"Owing to the large amount of feeling shown, I maintain that had the teams met on Saturday it would have led to a worse riot, and I fail to see what either club is to lose by the fixture being postponed for a few weeks. Referring to the charge made against Linton of having used foul language to, and of having struck, McMahon, I give it the most unqualified denial, and I may state that McMahon during the first half of the game threatened to do for Linton at the close of the match".

Before the second round of the Forfarshire Cup got under way, however, there was another ill-tempered incident at WestCraigiePark on 16th November, this time during a friendly between Our Boys and East End. Just before half-time, with Our Boys leading 2-1, the dark-blues inside-right Chalmers, for no apparent reason, kicked East End's McHardy in the stomach. The East End player then retaliated with a few hard kicks of his own.

"A scene of the wildest description now took place", reported the Dundee Courier, as a disgraceful fight broke out between several players of both sides. The battle was eventually broken up when Spalding, one of the East End half-backs, restrained Our Boys' McFarlane, in order to prevent him chasing and lashing out at the opposition players. The whole situation was not helped by a group of Our Boys supporters fuelling the altercation with provocative shouts from the comfort of their seats in the grandstand!

The match was eventually allowed to proceed, and a disappointing encounter, which was *"characterized throughout by roughness"*, eventually ended with the score 8-3 in favour of the home side.

The matter did not finish there, however, and at a subsequent meeting of the Forfarshire Football Association, four players; Our Boys' Chalmers and McFarlane and East End's Longair and McHardy, were severely censured for rough play.

In the second round of the Forfarshire Cup, Our Boys were drawn to face Forfar Athletic at WestCraigiePark, where the home side booked their place in the semi-final following a disappointing and largely uneventful match that ended 4-3 in favour of the dark-blues.

As for East End, the wise-men also made it through to the last four of the county competition without having kicked a ball. After having received a 'bye' in the first round, the Pitkerro Park men were handed a ticket to the semi-final following the withdrawal of second round opponents Lindertis, and their first actual involvement in the competition came on the last Saturday in December, a week after their Scottish Cup exit.

Despite having three regulars ruled out through injury, the wise-men raced to a three-goal half-time lead, but it has to be said that this tally might not have been so great had Harp's Mitchell not had to retire *"through his leg giving way"* just after the first goal was scored. The Harp defender returned to action at the start of the second half, but only lasted for a short period before having to leave the field for a second time.

East End then took full advantage of the situation by scoring another two goals to the delight of the majority of the large crowd, and progressed to the final of the county cup for the second year in a row with a 5-0 victory. A subsequent protest from Harp on the grounds that PitkerroPark was too short and narrow for a cup-tie, and that the goals were not of the proper size, was rejected by the Forfarshire Association.

Meanwhile, on adjacent WestCraigiePark, Our Boys were entertaining cup-holders Arbroath in the replay of the other semi-final. A week earlier, at Gayfield, the two sides had shared the honours in front of a bumper crowd of almost 4,000; a large contingent having made their way up the coast from Dundee. In that game, the dark-blues were on the verge of winning what had been an exciting encounter when the home side equalised with virtually the last kick of the ball.

Our Boys were determined not to let victory over the previous season's winners slip from their grasp for a second time, and swept Arbroath aside in the replayed match by five-goals-to-two. In doing so, the dark-blues had reached the final of the Forfarshire Cup for the first time in their history.

The final of the county competition between Our Boys and East End was played early in the new year, on 18th January 1890, at Harp's East Dock Street ground. Eagerly anticipated by followers of the participating sides as well as by other factions of the Dundee footballing fraternity, a crowd of over 6,000 turned out for the event.

The match also had the added incentive that, with neither side having previously won the tournament, a new name was going to be engraved on the trophy whatever the outcome.

With a strong breeze behind them, Our Boys opened the scoring in the early stages through a headed goal. East End tried desperately to hit back, and had the dark-blues goal under considerable pressure as the half progressed, but before half-time was called Our Boys had added a second point.

The wise-men started the second half in determined fashion, but despite having the lion's share of play and chances, could only secure one goal. When the referee blew the final whistle with the score standing 2-1 in favour of the dark-blues, jubilant celebrations broke out amongst the Our Boys' supporters. Their side had won the Forfarshire Cup!

However, a protest was subsequently lodged by East End claiming that they had been denied what had seemed a legitimate goal during the first half. The wise-men also alleged that Our Boys supporters had disrupted play by whistling, and had also encroached upon the field of play and interfered with the East End players. Initially, the protests were upheld by the Forfarshire Association, and the decision was taken to replay the final.

Following a long and bitter debate, which raged on for over a month, the matter was finally dropped when Our Boys threatened legal action against the Forfarshire Football Association. The decision to replay the final was overturned, and the result of the disputed match was allowed to stand. The name of Our Boys F.C. could finally be engraved on the trophy!

Just a week later, there was cause for further celebration at West Craigie Park when Our Boys' second string, the Rangers, won the Forfarshire Second Eleven Cup for a third time by beating their counterparts from Arbroath by a staggering eight-goals-to-nil!

The Burns Charity Cup, which was no longer organised and governed by the F.F.A, was organised under a slightly different format for the 1889/90 season than it had been in previous years. In order to maximize attendances, it was agreed that no two ties would be played on the same date, and that all the games would be played on Harp's East Dock Street ground.

The competition got under way on Saturday 22nd March 1890, when Wanderers disposed of Lochee by six-goals-to-nil. A fortnight later, in the other semi-final, East End recorded a 4-0 victory over Harp, who it has to be said were now but a shadow of the side they had been in previous seasons. These two clubs were then drawn to face each other in the first semi-final, with Our Boys facing Strathmore in the other tie.

On Wednesday 23rd April, in front of a large crowd at East Dock Street, East End lined up to face Wanderers for the right to play in the Burns Cup Final. The wise-men started the match in great form, and opened the scoring inside the first minute before racing to a 4-0 half-time lead. Wanderers tried desperately to come back into the game during the second half, but found they were no match for East End, who eventually ran out victors by six-goals-to-one.

In the second semi-final, between Our Boys and Strathmore on Wednesday 30th April at the same venue, another large crowd turned out to witness the action. Strathmore dominated the opening exchanges, and opened the scoring just a few minutes into the game through a well-taken header.

After weathering some further pressure, Our Boys eventually managed to create some chances of their own, but were denied on more than one occasion by the brilliance of the 'Strathie' goalkeeper. Before half-time, Strathmore had added a second point, and eventually scored a third goal fifteen minutes into the second half to put the result beyond doubt.

The final of the Burns Charity Cup between East End and Strathmore was played on Saturday 10th May, again at East Dock Street, where despite poor weather a crowd of just over 3,000 turned out to see which club was to be crowned champions of Dundee.

Although East End were expected to win, few if any of the spectators could have predicted the eventual winning margin.

The wise-men were aided in no small way by a first-half injury to Strathmore's Anderson, who was forced to retire, leaving the 'Strathie' with only ten men to play out the remainder of the game.

Leading 3-0 at half-time, East End showed their opponents no mercy during the second half, and notched up a further six goals against one solitary counter from Strathmore to win 9-1 and lift the Burns Cup for the first time.

The victory was not, however, to everyone's liking. In the following Monday's edition of the Evening Telegraph, a correspondent going by the nom-de-plume of 'Manly Football', expressed his disgust at the tactics that, in his opinion, had been used by East End to win the trophy.

It was his point of view that it was entirely due to the rough play meted out by the wise-men that Strathmore's Anderson had been injured to the extent that he had had to retire from the field, and that two other players had also been *"rendered useless for the remainder of the match"*. The writer then concluded that if East End wished to *"obtain respect in that circle to which they aspire, they had better set about mending their manners"*. The correspondent did not state in his letter which team he favoured, but it seems perfectly obvious that 'Manly Football was a regular patron at Rollo's Pier!

Both East End and Our Boys had every reason to be satisfied with how the 1889/90 season had turned out. Both clubs had landed silverware, and both clubs had won far more matches than they had lost over the course of the campaign. In addition, of the six clubs considered at that time to be the best in Dundee, they had by far the superior record.

Our Boys and the Wise Men, with both the Forfarshire Cup and the Burns Charity Cup in their respective trophy cabinets, could now rightfully claim to be the top two sides not only in Dundee but throughout Forfarshire!

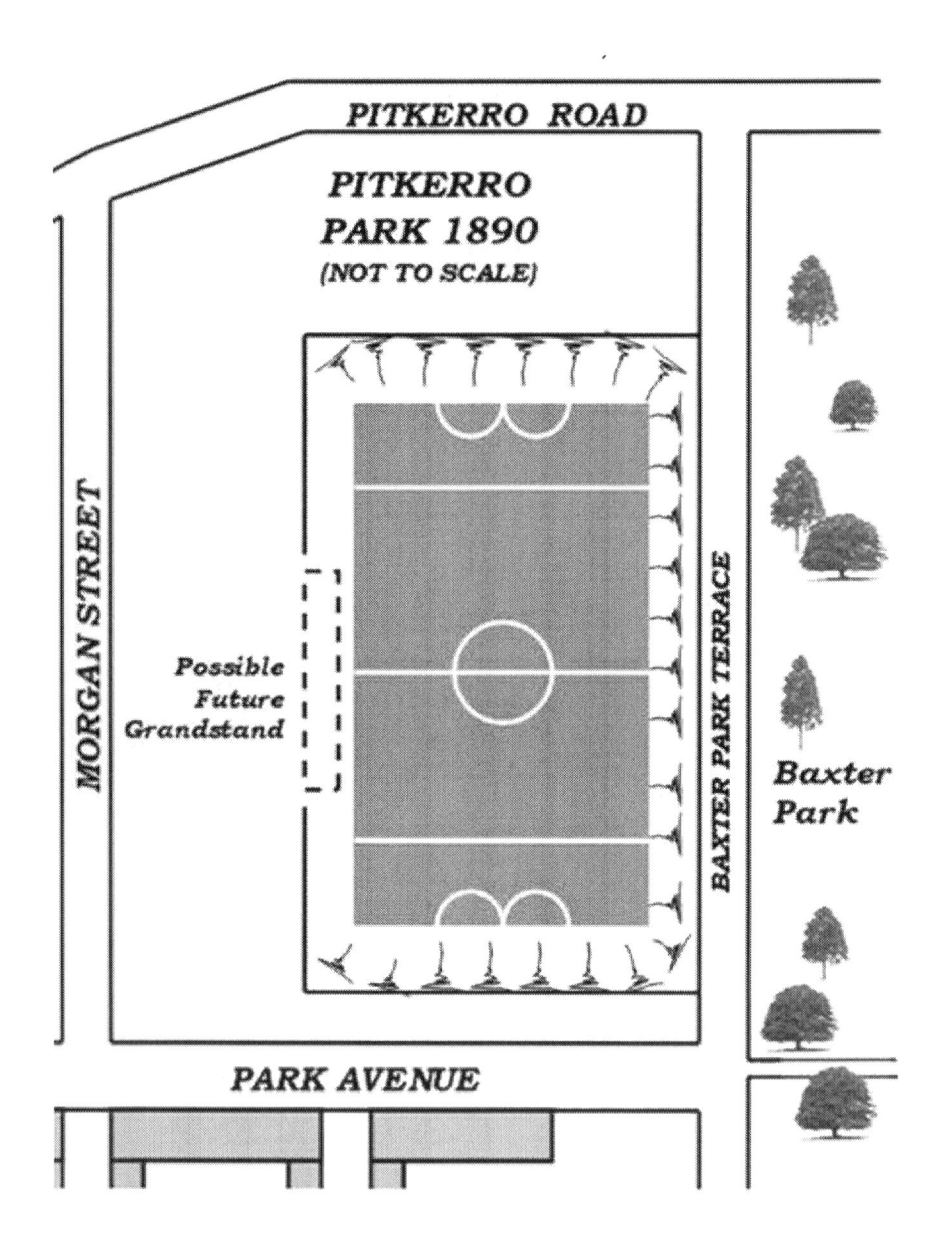

Pitkerro Park following the extensive improvements carried out during the summer of 1890, which included the building up of an embankment around three sides of the ground.

14

Our Boys Win 'The Double'

East End's achievement in reaching the latter stages of the Scottish Cup during season 1889/90 had proved the club's ability to compete with some of the country's best football clubs. This improvement in form meant that Pitkerro Park was now attracting larger crowds for competitive matches, but sadly the ground's facilities fell far short of what was required in order to accommodate the increased attendances in comfort, and this prompted the East End committee to investigate the possibility of moving to a bigger and better ground during the early months of 1890. When it became apparent towards the end of the 1889/90 season that no suitable ground was available, it was decided that the wisemen should remain at PitkerroPark and upgrade the ground to a more acceptable standard.

The necessary works were carried out during the summer of 1890 and, when the first home match of the season took place on 20th September, the crowd enjoyed a marked improvement in spectator facilities. Although Pitkerro Park was already a fully enclosed ground before the improvements, the paying spectators had, until now, been forced to watch the match from what was described as a 'ditch' that surrounded most of the pitch.

The extensive earthworks carried out prior to the 1890/91 season not only filled in the ditch, but provided a grass slope around the north, east and south sides, from which the game could be enjoyed in relative comfort. The club also invested in a new steel rope in order to keep the crowd away from the edge of the playing surface.

With East End also stating at this time that it was their intention to carry out further improvements to PitkerroPark as and when finances would allow, one can only assume that the embankment was only raised on three sides of the ground in order to leave space for the possible future erection of a grandstand along the western side.

The improved PitkerroPark was opened with an emphatic 9-1 victory over respected west of Scotland side Uddingston, and it certainly looked like the future was rosy for the wise-men!

One Dundee club, however, was now struggling to survive for want of a ground. Strathmore's lease on Rollo's Pier, which as previously stated was one of the more commodious grounds in the city, expired in March 1890, and the club was refused a renewal of their contract. The landlords, it transpired, had agreed to rent the land to the Magdalen Yard Tennis Club, whose intention it was to replace the football pitch with ten tennis courts. Within weeks of the announcement, Strathmore had been evicted, and were left desperately trying to find a new ground for the 1890/91 season.

Desperate attempts were made to enter into an agreement to share land with a local cycling club, but when this failed to materialise, Strathmore were forced to spend the entire 1890/91 season playing away from home or, when the need arose, borrow a ground from one of the other Dundee clubs.

As for Our Boys, the West Craigie men started the 1890/91 season in the same way they had ended the previous campaign, and kicked off with a 5-2 victory away to Cowdenbeath on 16th August before beating St Bernard's 5-4 in their first home match a week later. At the end of the month, Our Boys were invited to take part in an exhibition match against Third Lanark in Edinburgh, as part of the International Exhibition of Science, Art & Industry, which had been organised to commemorate the opening of the ForthRailwayBridge.

The match was played at the Meggetland recreation grounds, where a crowd of 4,000 were *"treated to a succession of interchanges, the scene of play changing with kaleidoscopic rapidity"*. Despite leading by a single goal at the half-time interval, the dark-blues eventually succumbed to the Glasgow side and went down by two-goals-to-one.

Our Boys' first competitive match of the season was played on Saturday 6th September, when Forfar Athletic were convincingly beaten 7-2 at StationPark in the first round of the Scottish Cup. When the draw for the second round was made, the dark-blues were handed a 'bye' into round three.

East End were due to play Strathmore at PitkerroPark on the same afternoon in the same competition, and a large crowd basked in warm sunshine eagerly awaiting the commencement of the cup-tie.

Only four Strathmore players showed up, however, and the East End committee had no other option but to refund the admission money to the disappointed spectators. One can only assume that the current plight of the Strathmore club, as mentioned earlier in this chapter, had instilled apathy amongst their playing staff.

The second round of the Scottish Cup saw East End drawn at home to St. Johnstone, and in front of another large crowd, many of whom had travelled from Perth, the wise-men eventually won a hard-fought game by four-goals-to-two.

In the third round, Our Boys and East End were drawn to face each other in the national competition for the second successive season.

The match was scheduled for West Craigie Park on 18th October 1890, where *"an immense crowd of spectators"* saw the home side gain revenge for their defeat at the hands of the wise-men at the same stage of the tournament exactly a year earlier, with a 4-0 victory.

Our Boys' reward was a fourth round home clash with Glasgow Celtic; a club that had made a huge impression on Scottish Football since its inception just a couple of years earlier, when they had reached the final of the Scottish Cup at the first time of asking. The Glasgow club tried desperately to gain home advantage by offering Our Boys a big financial guarantee to move the game west, but the dark-blues, keen to ensure that the match be witnessed by as many Dundee folk as possible, declined the offer.

The local football enthusiasts responded by turning out in their droves and, on 8th November 1890, an Our Boys record home crowd of over 6,000 paid to see the dark-blues take on one of the best teams in the land. For a while it looked like the home side might just be capable of recording a famous victory after centre-forward Grewar opened the scoring from a free kick, to which the crowd responded with a deafening roar.

With half-time approaching, however, Celtic scored three goals in rapid succession to take control of the match. Our Boys tried their best to get back into the game during the second forty-five minutes, but it was all in vain, and with no further scoring the Glasgow side ran out victors by three goals to one.

In the aftermath, it would appear that Our Boys were unhappy about the circumstances in which the Glasgow side had won the cup-tie and, at a meeting of the Our Boys committee on the following Monday, it was resolved to lodge a protest with the Scottish Football Association.

However, although the protest was posted that same evening, the letter was not received by the S.F.A. until 21:00 on Tuesday 11th November, missing the deadline for protests by three hours. Consequently, the protest was not read, and we have no way of knowing what Our Boys' complaint was actually about!

A further protest was then lodged claiming that clubs from the east of the country did not have the same geographical advantage when lodging an objection as the western clubs, who could simply hand in their protests directly to the S.F.A. office. That complaint also fell on deaf ears.

It would appear, however, that the skills of certain local players had not gone un-noticed during the clash with the Celtic. A few months later, when the international selection committee was preparing its squad for the Home International Championships, Our Boys' goalkeeper Gold, right-half Craig, right-wing Coupar and centre-forward Buttar were all invited for trials at HampdenPark. When the final selection of players to represent Scotland was made, however, every position on the field was once again occupied by players from the west of the country.

Meanwhile, East End embarked on their Forfarshire Cup campaign when they played host to Broughty on 25th October 1890 in the first round of the competition. An exciting encounter resulted in a 5-2 victory for the wise-men over a youthful Broughty side, for which they were rewarded with a home clash against Lochee United. For the record, Lochee F.C. had added the 'United' suffix to their name on the opening of their new ground at South Road just a week earlier.

On 22nd November, despite drizzling rain, another large crowd congregated on the PitkerroPark terraces for the second round of the county competition, and were treated to a one-sided display from the home side, who scored four goals without reply during the first half. Playing down the slope during the second forty-five minutes, the wise-men went one better and scored five times to win the tie by nine-goals-to-nil.

On the same afternoon, in front of *"a very large attendance of spectators"* at StationPark in Forfar, Our Boys, who had received a 'bye' in the first round, kicked off their Forfarshire Cup campaign against the local Athletic.

In a first half totally dominated by the cup holders, the dark-blues ran up a 6-0 lead before the interval, and it looked like the tie was as good as won. Forfar had other ideas, however, and with the wind at their backs scored four times in quick succession after the interval to reduce Our Boys' lead to two goals. Although the home side still had time to further reduce the leeway, they failed to use the wind to their best advantage and the cup holders held out to progress to the next stage of the competition.

When the names were drawn out of the hat for the semi-finals of the Forfarshire Cup, East End were handed yet another home tie, this time against Arbroath; whilst Our Boys were faced with a sixty-mile round trip to play Montrose at Links Park. If both clubs could safely negotiate their semi-final ties, then a mouth-watering repeat of the previous season's final was on the cards!

On the morning of Saturday 13th December, the Our Boys players and officials boarded the 11:30 train from TayBridge station bound for Montrose, accompanied by numerous jovial supporters, all highly excited at the possibility of progressing to the Forfarshire Cup final for a second successive season. With Montrose having never before reached the semi-final of the county competition, the local football fans turned out in their droves for the occasion, and by kick-off time LinksPark was filled to overflowing with followers of both sides.

It was the home supporters who had more reason to be cheerful when the half-time whistle sounded, however, with Montrose having broken the deadlock shortly before the interval. This only served to spark the cup holders into action, and the game was turned around with two goals scored in quick succession shortly after the re-start. There was no further scoring, and the dark-blues progressed to the final, although Montrose did try to have the result annulled at a following meeting of the Forfarshire Association on the grounds of rough play by Our Boys.

In the other semi-final, at PitkerroPark, East End played host to Arbroath, where a large contingent of travelling supporters helped boost the crowd to almost 4,000. It was the visitors who looked the more likely side during the opening exchanges, and the wise-men had the woodwork to thank for keeping the score blank.

The home players gradually worked their way into the game, however, and eventually broke the deadlock *"amid wild cheering"*. Arbroath hit back immediately to level the score, only for East End to immediately reply by stepping up a gear; and, following sustained pressure, they managed to reclaim the lead before the half-time whistle sounded.

In the second half, the wise-men took complete control of the game, and with *"dashing play"* scored an incredible seven times against one counter from the visitors to win by nine-goals-to-two!

East End had reached the final of the Forfarshire Cup for the third year in a row, but would they finally be able to claim the silverware that had so far eluded the club? With the final of the competition not due to take place until late January, the wise-men had several weeks to wait for the answer.

Strathmore, as stated earlier, were in dire straits at this time and, without a home ground, they were struggling to survive financially. They were not alone, however. In the early weeks of 1891, local rivals Wanderers declared that they were also suffering financial difficulties, and as a result they were evicted from their home ground, Morgan Park, after failing to pay the rent.

Wanderers were consequently forced to sell off all of their assets, including their grandstand, goal-posts, wire ropes, and 150 yards of perimeter fencing. Although the sale realised sufficient funds to clear off Wanderers' debt of £28 with a surplus of £5, they were now homeless, and unless a new ground could be found, they were in danger of folding.

In order to make a fresh start, Wanderers decided to re-establish themselves under the new name of Johnstone Wanderers, and eventually the club secured the tenancy of ClepingtonPark, the former home of both Our Boys and East End.

The eagerly anticipated final of the Forfarshire Cup eventually went ahead on Saturday 24th January 1891 at East Dock Street, where a sizeable crowd of almost 6,000 paid to see the action. Although clear and favourable weather greeted the teams and their supporters, the underfoot conditions were not suited to good football. With the snow and frost that had covered the ground on the eve of the match having now thawed, several puddles of water now covered the entire playing surface.

Following a sustained period of even play in the opening half-hour, during which both sides created chances, Our Boys eventually mastered the slippery conditions and scored three times before the referee blew for half-time.

It was at this stage, just after the teams had left the field, that it was discovered that an error had been made by the timekeeper, and that the first half had only lasted forty minutes. A great debate then ensued as to how the situation could be rectified, as the mistake could well give the eventual losing side ample reason to lodge a protest. Several solutions were considered, including a proposal to play out the remainder of the match as a friendly, and replay the final at a later date.

What was eventually agreed upon, however, was a rather strange solution, and one which has probably never been repeated in any other Association football match. When the two sides returned to the field following the interval, they were instructed to play in the same direction that they had been playing during the first half for five minutes, before turning around and immediately playing for a further forty-five minutes in the other direction!

Although East End managed to exert pressure on Our Boys' goal following the restart, during which time they scored twice to reduce the leeway to just one goal, the dark-blues took control once again and eventually ran out 6-2 winners to claim the Forfarshire Cup for a second successive year.

Following the match, the players and officials of both clubs retired to White's Tea Rooms in Commercial Street, where the chairman of the Forfarshire Football Association, Mr. Henry Bryan of Arbroath, made some rather interesting remarks during his commemorative speech.

It was Mr. Bryan's opinion that the Forfarshire Cup could not truly be considered the county championship, as to claim that title a team should have to play and beat every other team in the county. The chairman then went on to say that it was his intention to bring a motion before the Forfarshire Association that a league should be formed between all the clubs in the Association in order to decide the true champions.

Mr. Bryan concluded by adding that an invitation to join the competition should also be sent out to clubs in the north-east of Scotland. His comments were greeted with enthusiastic applause.

It was clear that the chairman's remarks had been influenced by the success of the Scottish League, inaugurated the previous year, and it now looked highly likely that a similar competition for clubs based north of the Firth of Tay would be formed sooner rather than later.

There was no such league tournament to occupy the local teams during the remainder of the current season, and once again the top Dundee sides turned their attentions to the

Burns Charity Cup. Prior to the tournament, however, some interesting comments were made at a meeting of the Burns Charity Football Association by a Mr. Spalding, who represented East End.

It was Mr. Spalding's opinion that only tea should be served following the Burns Cup ties, and that his club were totally opposed to the serving of liquor to the players at such meetings.

It was also his considered opinion that *"many people had the idea that football and general loose tone and loose habits went together, and the sooner this was shown to be incorrect the better"*. It was also proposed that all such post-match get-togethers should be held in Lamb's Temperance Hotel, where *"there could not even be the suspicion of drink"*. Mr. Spalding's motion was left open for discussion at a future meeting.

The Burns Charity Cup for season 1890/91, which was played under the same format as the previous season with all matches staged at East Dock Street, eventually got under way on 4th April when Harp defeated Lochee United 6-1 in miserable conditions. A fortnight later, Our Boys recorded an even more emphatic victory, when they thumped Strathmore, who were still struggling for survival, by eleven-goals-to-one.

The draw for the semi-finals paired Our Boys with Harp and East End with Johnstone Wanderers. The first of these ties was played between the latter two clubs at East Dock Street on Wednesday 29th April 1891, where cup holders East End were convincingly beaten in front of a large and vociferous gathering of spectators.

Exactly a week later, Our Boys faced Harp in the other semi in front of another big attendance, who were treated to a closely-fought encounter which eventually finished 2-1 in favour of the dark-blues.

The final of the Burns Cup between Our Boys and Johnstone Wanderers, which was scheduled for Saturday 16th May 1891, was once again an eagerly awaited event, and in anticipation of a huge crowd the Dundee Tramway Company arranged for a frequent horse-drawn 'bus service to operate between the High Street and East Dock Street.

Despite a *"bitter wind from the north"*, a crowd of almost 6,000 paid to see the action, and they were not disappointed. Both sides served up an exciting tussle, described as *"the most exciting match that has been played between Dundee clubs for a considerable time"*, in which Our Boys dominated the first half and scored three goals without reply.

During the second forty-five minutes, however, the roles were reversed, and Wanderers scored three times to level the game, with their equalising goal coming in the dying minutes.

A week later, the teams met at the same venue to settle the tie, and once again a crowd of around 6,000 turned out for the event. An exciting match ensued, and towards the end of an evenly contested first half, during which both sides had registered two goals, Our Boys gained the advantage with a third just before the interval.

Wanderers tried hard to equalise during the early stages of the second half, and almost succeeded on several occasions, but Our Boys held firm, and eventually put the game out reach with a further two goals before Wanderers added a late consolation. Eight years after the inauguration of the competition, Our Boys had finally managed to land the Burns Charity Cup!

With both the Forfarshire Cup and the Burns Cup in the West Craigie trophy cabinet, there could be no doubt that season 1890/91 had been the most successful to date for Our Boys. In addition to the silverware won by the club, the dark-blues had also reached the fourth round of the Scottish Cup and, as stated earlier, four of their players had been considered for international duty.

East End, on the other hand, had no trophies to show for their efforts over the season, but the club could be justifiably proud of having reached the third round of the Scottish Cup and the final of the Forfarshire Cup.

There could be no doubt that the local football clubs were steadily improving, but what was really required now, in order to keep the momentum going, was regular competitive matches. The idea of such games being played between the local teams in the form of a league competition was first mooted by Forfarshire Football Association chairman Henry Bryan during his speech following the final of the Forfarshire Cup, and the idea had grown in popularity over the weeks that followed. The Northern League was about to be born!

15

The Northern League

As previously mentioned, towards the end of the 1890/91 season the Association football clubs based north of the Firth of Tay were now largely in favour of forming a league competition in order to provide regular competitive matches.

With this in mind, club representatives from teams in Dundee, Aberdeen, Perth, Forfar, Montrose and Arbroath met on Saturday 14th March 1891 in Dundee to discuss the formation of such a competition, and the Northern League was inaugurated.

The Scottish League, which had just completed its first season, had been hailed a huge success. The competition had gone right to the wire, with Dumbarton and Rangers eventually being declared joint champions of the ten-team league, and it was hoped that the Northern League would also result in a closely-fought and exciting competition.

Membership of the Scottish League had been increased to twelve clubs for season 1891/92, and initially it was proposed to form the Northern League with the same number of sides.

The twelve teams that applied for membership of the new competition were Dundee's East End, Our Boys, Johnstone Wanderers and Harp; fellow Forfarshire Association clubs Forfar Athletic, Arbroath and Montrose; northern clubs Aberdeen, Orion (Aberdeen) and Victoria United (Aberdeen); and Perth clubs St. Johnstone and FairCity.

In the event, however, the league was inaugurated with only eight teams after FairCity, Johnstone Wanderers, Orion and Victoria United were voted out by the league committee.

Missing from the list of proposed clubs was Strathmore, who were still without a home ground and in danger of going out of existence completely. Consequently, in August 1891, a meeting was called *"of those favourable to the re-organisation of the Strathmore Football Club"*, to be held in the City's Albert Coffee House.

The meeting was well attended and, after having considered Strathmore's current situation, those present resolved to press ahead and leave no stone unturned in their search to secure a new home ground for the forthcoming season. Eventually, the club decided to take up an offer of land from Messrs. Cox, owners of the Scott Street Linen Works, and without further delay Strathmore made the necessary arrangements to get the new ground in order.

On the final day of the month, through the medium of the local press, Strathmore were finally able to release the following statement:

"We are now in a position to state that the Strathmore have secured a park situated on the south side of Scott Street. Men are now at work getting the ground in order, and the stripes will meet the Kirriemuir on LogiePark on Saturday in the first round of the Scottish Cup ties".

On Saturday 5th September 1891, Strathmore's new LogiePark, which was located where Logie Avenue exists today, was officially opened amidst much ceremony prior to their Scottish Cup first round tie with Kirriemuir, who proceeded to spoil the party by defeating the home side by seven-goals-to-three.

Strathmore were not the only side moving in to a new home. Despite having invested a considerable amount of money on PitkerroPark at the beginning of the previous season, East End decided that their ground was not up to the standard required for the Northern League and the anticipated increase in attendances.

One other deciding factor was that there was now an increased demand for new housing in Dundee, and it was only a matter of time before the owners of the ground on which PitkerroPark was situated would decide to sell the land to housing developers.

Before the new season got under way, East End secured a lease on a new purpose-built sports and athletics stadium on the banks of the Tay, a little to the east of the shipbuilding yards on the south side of the Dundee to Arbroath railway line.

Officially named the Dundee Athletic Grounds, East End's new stadium was more commonly referred to as Carolina Port, and was opened for football amidst great ceremony on 22nd August 1891 with a match against the intriguingly named Glasgow side I Zingari, which consisted mainly of players from Queen's Park football club. Despite wet weather conditions, a sizeable crowd turned out for the game, and were treated to an entertaining encounter that ended in favour of the home side by three-goals-to-one.

Less than a year after the wise-men had vacated Pitkerro Park, construction work started on the development of the four-storey tenements that stand today in Baldovan Terrace, Baxter Park Terrace and Park Avenue.

CarolinaPort was by far East End's best home ground to date, being fully enclosed and boasting a sizeable grandstand as well as a running track. As their name would suggest, the Athletic Grounds Company, from whom the stadium was leased, also used the venue for athletics and cycle meetings.

The eagerly-anticipated Northern League finally got under way on 12th September 1891, and East End's first ever fixture in the competition was played against Forfar Athletic at Station Park, where full points were taken thanks to a first-half penalty kick that proved to be the only goal of the game.

A match in progress at Carolina Port, East End's home ground from 1891 to 1893 and future home of both Strathmore and Dundee F.C.

Strathmore in season 1891/92, shortly after the club had been saved from extinction.

A week later, Our Boys played their first Northern League fixture, also against Forfar Athletic, who they beat convincingly by six-goals-to-two in front of a sizeable crowd at WestCraigiePark. Further victories for East End then followed, including an emphatic 5-0 victory over Our Boys at West Craigie, and at the beginning of November the wise-men sat proudly at the top of the Northern League table with a 100% record.

Of course both East End and Our Boys also had their Scottish Cup ties to play, and the wise-men successfully negotiated the first two rounds of the competition with a 3-1 victory over Forfar Athletic at StationPark followed by a 7-1 thumping of Pitlochry side Vale of Atholl.

Our Boys, on the other hand, were knocked out by local rivals Harp in round one. Following an exciting 4-4 draw at East Dock Street in front of what was described as *"the largest crowd which has turned out to witness a football match in Dundee for many a day"*, the dark-blues were beaten 2-0 at home in the replay.

The third round saw East End drawn at home to Harp on 17th October, and the first-ever Scottish Cup tie to be staged at Carolina Port ended all-square at a goal apiece. A week later, East End successfully negotiated the replay with a 2-0 victory, but the match ended in controversy when several East End supporters, sensing that victory was within their grasp, encroached on to the running track at the side of the East Dock Street pitch.

Harp subsequently protested to the Scottish Football Association on the grounds that the aforementioned supporters had interfered with play; that the referee *"was not proficient"*; that the game had been ended prematurely with five minutes still on the clock; and that the East End linesman had been coaching his players rather than carrying out his official duties.

The referee was consequently asked to give his version of events, and in a letter to the S.F.A. he vehemently refuted the claims, and added that as he was in possession of two watches the match could not possibly have ended prematurely. The protest was thrown out, and East End progressed to the next round.

In round four of the Scottish Cup, East End were drawn at home to face Monkcastle, who hailed from Kilwinning in Ayrshire. However, at this time there was a rule which stated that no team should have to travel more than 100 miles to fulfil a Scottish Cup tie.

As the distance from Kilwinning to Dundee exceeded 100 miles, the match had to be re-located to a neutral venue roughly equidistant to both clubs, and Stirling was chosen as the location to host the tie.

The match went ahead on Saturday 7th November on the ground of King's Park Football Club, where, despite putting up a good performance on the day, the wise-men eventually succumbed to their Ayrshire opponents, who were by all accounts a strong, physical team.

Undeterred by two early goals from Monkcastle, East End fought their way back and levelled the match shortly after the interval, but almost immediately the Ayrshire side scored four goals in quick succession to establish a commanding lead.

The Dundee side tried their best to rectify the situation, but with former Scotland international Johnnie Allan commanding the Monkcastle defence, their task was always going to be a difficult one. When the final whistle eventually sounded, the wise-men retired defeated by six-goals-to-three.

Meanwhile, Our Boys were enjoying better luck in the Forfarshire Cup ties. In the first round, played on the last day of October, Arbroath were beaten at Gayfield to earn the dark-blues a home clash with Harp in the second round.

On Saturday 21st November, West Craigie Park was *"taxed almost to its limit"* for the tie, which was won by seven goals without reply.

East End were also having a favourable run in the county competition, and in front of an *"eager crowd"* at Carolina Port they defeated Johnstone Wanderers by four goals to one in the first round. In round two, the wise-men were handed a home tie against Broughty Ferry, which went ahead in miserable conditions on Saturday 28th November.

With a gale-force wind and incessant rain drenching the supporters who were lining the ropes at the commencement of the match, the East End committee generously offered the wet and shivering spectators a free seat in the grandstand.

Despite playing into the gale during the first half, East End ran up a three-goal lead before heading in for their half-time cup of tea. As the wind and rain was going to be at their backs during the second half, it was expected that the wise-men would add considerably to their tally, but their opponents had other ideas.

Three goals behind, soaked to the skin, and faced with the daunting task of having to play into the wind and rain for a further forty-five minutes, the Broughty players decided that enough was enough. They scratched from the competition and headed for home!

The semi-final of the Forfarshire Cup paired East End with Our Boys at West Craigie Park where, after having been postponed due to a frozen pitch on 12th December, the match went ahead a week later. East End kicked off with a slight wind in their favour, and following some slick passing registered the first goal in the opening minutes.

The home side fought back, and when the half-time whistle sounded the score was level at a goal apiece.

Although Our Boys created several chances during the second half, the East End defence held firm, and eventually the wise-men scored another two points to run out victors by three-goals-to-one.

The wise-men had made it through to the final of the county competition for a fourth successive season. Would this be the year that East End's name would finally be engraved on the silverware? Only Montrose now stood between them and their first-ever lifting of the Forfarshire Cup.

Unfortunately, it was not to be. On Saturday 23rd January 1892, East End and Montrose lined up at the neutral venue of West Craigie Park in front of a crowd of 5,000 to determine the destination of the county trophy, but the match was played out in controversial circumstances. A special train had been arranged to convey the Montrose party and their supporters to Dundee, but owing to its late arrival, the game could not start at the agreed kick-off time of 2:45.

Play did eventually get under way fifteen minutes late, but the knock-on effect this had was that the match was completed in near-darkness, at which time East End were desperately trying to get back on level terms. Before full-time was called, left-back Brown, the East End captain, complained to the referee that the match could not continue owing to the poor light. His protest fell on deaf ears, and when the final whistle sounded the 'Gable Endies' were five-goals-to-three in front.

The matter did not rest there, however, and when the players and officials of both clubs retired to Mr White's Tea Rooms in Commercial Street for supper after the match, the presentation of the trophy was withheld pending an official protest from the wise-men regarding the late arrival of the Montrose team.

At a meeting of the Forfarshire Association, held a few days later, the appeal was heard, and the referee, Mr Gamble, was asked to give his version of events.

Any hopes that East End had that the result of the match would be overturned were well and truly dashed when the match official stated that he was in no doubt that game had been played out in plenty of light. And, as if to rub salt in the wound, Mr Gamble went on to state:

"Never in all my experience of refereeing football matches have I been subjected to such disgraceful treatment as I received at the hands of the East End club. If I were to repeat to the Association what was expressed to me by five individual members, I think the Association would have no hesitation in suspending them".

East End had failed yet again to win the Forfarshire Cup, but they were still very much in the running for the inaugural Northern League championship, as were Our Boys. At the beginning of December, the wise-men were still in pole position, albeit on goal average, having won four and lost only one of the five games played. Tucked in behind East End were Montrose and Our Boys, also on eight points, with Arbroath a point behind in fourth place.

The lead was subsequently relinquished to Montrose, but on Boxing Day 1891 East End were presented with a chance to regain pole position when they headed north to take on the league leaders at LinksPark. On the morning of the match, however, a problem arose. With the team assembled at Dundee railway station and about to board the train for Montrose, it was brought to the attention of club officials that goalkeeper Fotheringham had failed to appear; his employers having refused permission for the player to finish his Saturday morning shift in time to catch the train.

As luck would have it, a former player by the name of Reid was spotted at the station, and was hurriedly recruited to play in goal. Although he was not actually a goalkeeper, Reid stated that he had played for no other team within the previous fortnight, which made him eligible under league rules.

As one would have expected, the substitute 'keeper was not up to the task, and the Gable-Endies won by five-goals-to-three to extend their lead at the top of the table. The wise-men returned to Dundee to lick their wounds, oblivious to the fact that they had not heard the last of their decision to field former player Reid in goal; a decision that was to have serious repercussions as the league season reached its latter stages.

Both East End and Our Boys were still in a challenging position in the league table at the end of January 1892, with table-toppers Montrose having a two-point lead over the wise-men, and a four-point lead over the dark-blues.

The 'Gable Endies' had, however, played two games more than East End, and three games more than Our Boys. With these 'games in-hand', and with several league fixtures remaining, there was still everything to play for.

Our Boys, however, were going to have to improve discipline on the field of play if they wanted to be taken seriously as title challengers. During a 'friendly' against Lochee United at South Road Park in early January, with two inches of snow covering the ground, fighting broke out when Our Boys' forward Grewar decided to pelt Lochee's Haxton with a snowball. In retaliation, Haxton threw a punch at Grewar.

The referee eventually regained control, and the match was allowed to progress, although several players were, in the words of the match official: *"in a rather touchy mood, and were inclined to tactics partly frolicsome and partly pugilistic"*. Eventually, however, the match boiled over once again when Lochee's Scotland tripped Our Boys' Erentz, who retaliated, and *"a scene of general disorder ensued"*.

The crowd then leapt over the ropes to join in the melee, at which point *"numerous free fights and general rioting"* broke out. The referee, who later reported that *"a scene of general disorder ensued, players and spectators being mixed together in one wild, seething mass"*, had no other option but to abandon the match.

In the aftermath, both Grewar and Erentz of Our Boys, along with Lochee's Haxton, were suspended for one month.

Back on league duty in early February, the under-strength Our Boys were made to pay for their indiscipline when they lost 5-2 away to leaders Montrose, followed by a draw with Arbroath, which saw the dark-blues slip down the table. Two home victories were to follow, however, against St. Johnstone and Aberdeen, and at the beginning of March Our Boys' challenge was starting to get back on track.

East End weren't having it all their own way either as the championship race entered its final stages, and their title hopes were severely dented by a 6-1 hammering at the hands of near-neighbours Harp. The wise-men bounced back, however, and a home victory over league leaders Montrose followed by an impressive 5-1 success away to Arbroath saw the club draw level on points at the top of the Northern League by early March.

But East End's joy was short-lived. Fearing that the Northern League championship was slipping away from them, Montrose decided to protest about the wise-men having fielded an unsigned player in goal when the two clubs had met at Links Park back in December 1891. Despite the fact that over two months had passed since that defeat, Montrose brought it to the attention of the Northern League committee on 12th March that East End had used *"an ineligible player"*, the man in question being Reid, the goalkeeper, who had turned out for junior team West Ferry Athletic in the days leading up to the game. Following a heated discussion on the matter, a motion was put forward by Mr. Williamson, of Our Boys, that the wise-men be deducted two points for an infringement of league rules, despite the fact that East End had lost the game in any case. It is perhaps no coincidence that Our Boys' challenge for the league championship stood to benefit greatly from the proposed points deduction!

The motion was carried by three votes to two, and East End dropped to third place in the table, two points behind Montrose and one point behind Our Boys. Despite this setback, the wise-men fought their way back to the top of the table just a week later with a resounding 8-0 victory over Aberdeen at CarolinaPort, with leaders Montrose suffering a surprise 6-2 defeat at Forfar.

At this stage, Our Boys were sitting just a point behind the top two in third place, but had played a game less than East End and three games less than Montrose. If the dark-blues could win their remaining four matches then the league title would be theirs. In their very next league match, however, on 9th April, Our Boys suffered a humiliating defeat at the hands of bottom club Aberdeen!

The nerves were also creeping in to East End's performances, and in back to back league matches against St. Johnstone the spoils were shared in a 1-1 draw at Perth followed by a narrow 2-1 victory at Carolina Port in a nervous performance in which, according to the press report, *"more wretched fumbling and shooting has seldom been seen amongst the East End fronts"*.

With just one game to play, East End were still top of the league, and couldn't now be caught by Montrose, who also had one match remaining but were three points behind. Our Boys, on the other hand, were four points off the lead, but had three games to play. In order to win the Northern League, the dark-blues were going to have to take full points from their remaining fixtures and hope that the wise-men dropped at least a point in their one remaining match.

On the last day of April, Our Boys faced Arbroath at West Craigie Park, where a thrilling match finished in favour of the dark-blues by the odd-goal-in-nine; with the winner coming late in the game.

On the following Wednesday, full points were taken from Harp at the same venue with a one-sided 6-1 victory, which meant that Our Boys and East End now shared pole position with each team having one game to play.

On Saturday 7th May, in front of a large crowd and in weather that was described as *"all that could be desired"*, East End beat Forfar Athletic 2-0 at Carolina Port thanks to two second-half goals.

With Our Boys not due to play their last league match, against Montrose, until the following Saturday, the wise-men were now faced with nervous wait of seven days before the outcome of the race for the league title would be known.

A week later, Our Boys demolished Montrose 6-1 at West Craigie Park to draw level once again with East End at the top of the table. Although East End still had the better goal difference, having scored 44 and conceded 22 against Our Boys 56 goals for and 39 against, such statistics were not taken into consideration when league championships were being decided back in the late 1800's.

In order to decide the winners of the first-ever Northern League championship, it was decided that a play-off match should take place on Wednesday 25th May 1892 at Harp's East Dock Street ground. However, two days before the match was due to be played, East End intimated that they were refusing to take part as they reckoned that they had won the league championship fairly and squarely over the course of the season. The club further stated that they were prepared to take legal action in order to secure possession of the trophy.

The Northern League committee refused to recognise East End as champions, and re-scheduled the play-off for Tuesday 31st May. The wise-men still refused to participate, however, and following further debate it was decided that the very first

Northern League championship should be shared after East End agreed to drop their threat of legal action.

In the midst of the Northern League dispute, there was still the matter of the annual Dundee charity tournament to be played for. As the Dundee Burns Association was no longer responsible for organising the competition, a new organization called the Dundee Charity Football Association was inaugurated, and a new trophy, the Dundee Charity Football Shield, was introduced.

Unlike previous years, only four teams were invited to take part in the tournament; namely Our Boys, East End, Johnstone Wanderers and Harp. It would appear that, following the inception of the Northern League, interest in the charity competition had waned somewhat, and enthusiasm seemed to be somewhat lacking in the newspaper reports that followed the matches played.

East End and Johnstone Wanderers got the contest under way at East Dock Street on Saturday 21st May, where a relatively uneventful match ended in favour of the wise-men by the odd-goal-in-five. A week later, at the same venue, Our Boys knocked Harp out of the competition by four-goals-to-nil, to set up a mouth-watering clash with East End in the first-ever Dundee Charity Football Shield final.

On Saturday 4th June 1892, a large crowd turned out at East Dock Street for the final of the tournament, where they were treated to a fast and furious game in which five first-half goals were scored; three for East End and two for Our Boys. In the second half, despite several goalmouth incidents, there was no further scoring, and the Dundee Charity Shield ended up in the East End trophy cabinet. Although the winning of this trophy in no way made up for the wise-men being denied the Northern League championship, it was still a satisfying victory over the side that had, in effect, cost them that honour.

16

The Lure of Professionalism

For the 1892/93 season, membership of the Northern League was increased to ten clubs following the admission of Johnstone Wanderers and Perth side Fair City Athletic.

Our Boys kicked off their league campaign with a home match against St. Johnstone on 20th August and, after having scored a remarkable seven goals without reply during the first half, it looked like a 'cricket score' was on the cards. The visitors refused to give up, and with the WestCraigiePark slope in their favour during the second forty-five minutes, they scored five times. On chances created, they were perhaps unfortunate not to rescue at least a point from the match!

The big talking point amongst the spectators at this game, however, was not the remarkable score-line, but the fact that only two Our Boys' players from the previous season were in the side for the opening league match. As for St. Johnstone, they too had several players from their previous campaign missing. The reason for the depletion in both teams was due entirely to the exodus of players at this time to sign for professional sides in England, where professionalism had been legalised some seven years earlier. Initially, in order to prevent Scottish players abandoning their clubs and migrating south, the English Football Association put 'residential restrictions' in place.

However, when these restrictions were lifted in 1889, the mass exodus of players to English professional clubs began. By 1892, the number of players heading south had reached such a level it was becoming a serious concern for the well-being of the game in Scotland.

East End also kicked off their Northern League campaign on Saturday 20th August 1892 with a trip to face Aberdeen.

Although the wise-men had also lost some players to professional clubs from south of the border, the side they fielded for the opening game was largely along the same lines as that which had ended the previous season, and a 1-0 victory in the 'Granite City' was the outcome.

The fact that Our Boys had lost the nucleus of their team to professionalism, whereas East End had not, became increasingly apparent over the following weeks. In their second league match of the season, the dark-blues were beaten at Forfar, after which the Dundee Courier commented that the Our Boys' team *"showed unmistakable signs of the depredations of the English agent, there being only a few of last year's eleven present"*.

The West Craigie side continued to struggle as the weeks progressed, and league victories were few and far between. East End, on the other hand, were reaping the benefits of having managed to retain most of their team, and won their first six Northern League matches, including a 5-1 thumping of Our Boys at West Craigie Park. It was to be the beginning of December before the wise-men dropped their first point, when the honours were shared in a 3-3 draw with Johnstone Wanderers at CarolinaPort.

The early rounds of the 1892/93 Scottish Cup were also played during the first weeks of the season, and East End comfortably beat Arbroath Wanderers 4-1 in the first round at CarolinaPort on 3rd September. The wise-men came a cropper in round two, however, when they were surprisingly beaten convincingly at home by Forfar Athletic at the end of the month.

Our Boys fared better in the national competition, and opened their campaign with a 4-3 home victory over Lochee United.

In the second round, the dark-blues made the long trip to Aberdeen, where, at Central Park, Kittybrewster, they defeated Orion by four-goals-to-two.

The third round saw Our Boys drawn to face Dunblane at West Craigie on 15th October, where, on a cold and stormy afternoon, the home forwards failed to convert the many chances created, and a 2-2 draw was the outcome. A week later, the dark-blues travelled west for the replay, and after building a two-goal lead during the first half it looked like they were destined for round four. Dunblane came back strongly, however, and, after managing to square the match before half-time, went on to score another three during the second period to win by five-goals-to-two.

In the Forfarshire Cup, Our Boys failed to get past the first round thanks to a humbling 5-0 defeat away to holders Montrose. East End, on the other hand, fared better in the county competition. After sharing the honours away to Lochee United in the first round, the wise-men confidently disposed of the suburban club with a 7-1 replay victory at CarolinaPort.

In round two, East End were handed another away tie, this time against Brechin at Montrose Street Park, where the match was all but over after just ten minutes, at which point the wise-men were already three goals ahead. Although the home side tried their best to come back into the game, they were no match for the visitors, who eventually scored ten to Brechin's one.

The semi-final of the Forfarshire Cup saw East End drawn to face Harp at East Dock Street, and this tie eventually went ahead on Saturday 17th December after having been postponed a week earlier due to heavy snow. Before the kick-off, few of the spectators in the sizeable crowd gave the once-powerful Harp much of a chance against the side who were currently sweeping all before them.

The home side defied the odds, however, and at half-time were two goals ahead against an East End side who were described by the press as looking like *"a beaten team"* long before the first period had come to an end. In the second-half, the wise-men were rarely in the game, and eventually went down by five-goals-to-two.

East End were, by now, a highly respected side far beyond the local area, and with top class ground facilities at their disposal they were able to attract a high calibre of opposition to Dundee for challenge matches.

One such club was Sunderland, who had won the English League championship the previous season, and were well on their way to retaining the title when they lined up to face East End at CarolinaPort on the afternoon of Monday 10th October 1892.

There was great excitement throughout the city at the prospect of such a respected and successful team playing in Dundee, and a crowd of almost 8,000 paid to see the action. The Evening Telegraph, reporting on the match later that evening, commented:

"Sunderland made their debut before a Dundee audience on Carolina Port Grounds this afternoon. All lovers of football know Sunderland by reputation as being the leading Club in England, but few Dundonians had ever seen the combination on the football field, and it was not to be wondered therefore that nearly an hour before the advertised time for starting crowds were seen wending their way to the ground. By noon the enclosure was surrounded right round about two deep, and still the crowd was coming in. When the game started, punctually at 12.30, there could not be less than 8,000 spectators present".

Included in the Sunderland side was former Arbroath goalkeeper Ned Doig, a Scotland internationalist, who received a hearty cheer as the teams made their way on to the park.

The legendary goalkeeper Ned Doig, who was capped six times for Scotland. He started his senior career with Arbroath before going on to play for Blackburn Rovers, Sunderland and Liverpool.

Indeed, ten of the Sunderland side were Scotsmen, all of whom had learned the game north of the border; another example of how professionalism in England was draining Scotland of its football talent. As one would expect, East End were no match for an English professional side of such calibre, and lost by six-goals-to-two.

The wise-men then went on to host Stoke City, then described as holding a *"prominent place in the English League table"*, as part of their New Year programme on 3rd January 1893, when the honours were shared in a 2-2 draw in front of 6,000 at Carolina Port.

Back on Northern League duty, East End maintained their unbeaten record at the end of January with a 4-2 victory over Montrose at LinksPark. Our Boys indifferent form, on the other hand, continued, and a heavy league defeat at home to Harp severely dented any hopes the club may have still been harbouring that a title challenge could be made.

Victories over both Arbroath and Aberdeen in late January 1893, however, moved the dark-blues back into third place in the table with eleven points from ten games. Our Boys were now just four points adrift of table-toppers East End, and three points behind second-placed Arbroath, but having played two games more than the league leaders it was still highly unlikely that either of the top two could be caught.

At the beginning of February, East End's superiority over Our Boys was justified with a three-nil home victory over the dark-blues. It now looked very much like the title race was to be between the wise-men and Arbroath, and just a few weeks later the West Craigie side had completely dropped out of the running.

Things went from bad to worse for the dark-blues on Thursday 16th March 1893 when, at around eleven in the morning, the residents of the dwellings around

WestCraigiePark noticed smoke coming from the direction of the ground.

Closer inspection revealed that fire had broken out in the grandstand, on the west side of the park, and the local Fire Brigade was immediately summoned. Although they quickly arrived on the scene, they could do nothing to save the wooden structure; the entire northern half of which was completely ablaze. For the foreseeable future, teams playing at WestCraigiePark would have to change in a wooden shed at the northern end of the ground!

East End and Arbroath remained neck-and-neck in the race for the league championship, and by mid-March both clubs were sitting on twenty points, with the wise-men still in pole position and unbeaten after eleven matches. They also had the added advantage of having two games in hand.

However, following a surprise home defeat to Aberdeen, top spot in the league table was surrendered to Arbroath.

East End bounced back with victories over Harp and Johnstone Wanderers, but when Arbroath emerged victorious in the top-of-the-table clash at Gayfield in early April, it looked like the 1892/93 title race would be going to the wire.

Very little separated the sides as the end of the season approached, but with just two league fixtures remaining, East End would be assured of the title if full points could be taken from both matches. The first of these was against Montrose at CarolinaPort on Saturday 6th May and, with so much at stake, it was perhaps not surprising when tempers flared. Following a goal-less first half, during which Montrose, with a strong wind at their backs, had pounded the East End goal to no avail, the home side scored twice in quick succession just after the interval to take control of the game.

NORTHERN LEAGUE CHAMPIONSHIP

	Played	W.	L.	D.	For.	Agst.	Pts.
East End	11	9	0	2	40	12	20
Arbroath	13	10	3	0	49	32	20
Montrose	13	7	4	2	58	37	16
Forfar Athletic	13	7	5	1	49	40	15
Johnstone Wanderers	11	4	4	3	34	35	11
Our Boys	13	5	7	1	40	57	11
Aberdeen	13	4	7	2	41	52	10
Harp	10	4	5	1	42	31	9
St. Johnstone	10	3	6	1	30	34	7
Fair City Athletic	13	0	12	1	14	67	1

A win counts 2 points; a draw 1 point.

The Northern League table as it stood on 11th March 1893, when it looked very much like East End were shortly to become Northern League champions!

Montrose tried hard to hit back, but when centre-forward Murray was brought down by a hefty challenge in front of the East End goal, the player retaliated by having a kick at East End centre-half Longair.

All hell then broke loose when, as the East End players surrounded Murray in an attempt to calm him down, the Montrose supporters invaded the field led by club trainer Hunter who, wielding a stick, dealt Longair a heavy blow.

With the mob in hot pursuit, the East End man sought refuge in the grandstand, but to no avail as the angry Montrose supporters and players followed him in, and the feud continued amongst the seated spectators.

The referee then appealed to the players to return to the field of play and re-start the game, but when they refused he had no other option than to abandon the match and declare East End winners by two goals to nil.

There was now just one game to play, and if Harp could be defeated at East Dock Street in the final match, then the Northern League championship would be East End's.

Supporters of the wise-men would have to wait a fortnight for that mouth-watering clash, however, as the following Saturday, 13th May, had been set aside for the final of the Dundee Charity Shield, also to be played at East Dock Street. East End had reached the final of the tournament by overcoming Harp in the semi-final at the end of April. For the second year in a row, their opponents were to be Our Boys, who defeated Johnstone Wanderers in the other semi-final.

In perfect weather and in front of a large and enthusiastic crowd, both sides served up a thrilling match, with chances aplenty at either end of the park. It was the wise-men who made the most of those chances, and when the half-time whistle sounded they were three goals ahead.

A fourth goal shortly after the interval as good as put the result beyond doubt, and despite a spirited second half rally from the dark-blues, one of the fastest and most exciting games seen in Dundee that season ended 4-2 in favour of East End.

The wise-men were now confident that they were more than capable of doing the business against Harp in the final league match of the season, and all associated with the club were certain that the Northern League Championship Trophy would soon be sitting proudly alongside the Dundee Charity Shield in the CarolinaPort trophy cabinet.

However, on Saturday 20th May 1893, in front of a huge crowd, the wise-men let their supporters down with a nervous performance, and went down by four-goals-to-two, much to the disgust of the reporter from the Dundee Courier, who lamented:

"East End have disappointed their supporters. After keeping at the top of the league for most of the season, and in fact all last season, to fail in their last match when the championship was within their grasp, thus giving the Arbroath the honour of heading the list and securing the flag, is not much to their credit".

After having promised so much during an eventful season, the wise-men were once again left feeling bitterly disappointed when the season finally drew to a close.

As for Our Boys, their league campaign also finished disappointingly, with just fifteen points won from eighteen games played; a record which saw the dark-blues finish third from bottom, one point ahead of St. Johnstone and fourteen points in front of bottom club Fair City Athletic.

17

The Merger of Our Boys and East End

Controversial developments in Scottish football during the latter part of the 1892/93 season were about to cause sweeping changes throughout the country. After having been spoken about for some time, professionalism was finally accepted by the Scottish Football Association in May 1893, and the following extract, taken from the 'Scottish Referee', gives a clear indication on how this development was to affect the local teams:

"What the result of the new state of affairs will be in the North nobody can yet tell, though to those who have been watching events some things are plain enough. In the Dundee district all the clubs that can afford it will go in now for the openly paid player. As matters stand at present, however, there are too many senior clubs for all to pay, and amalgamation will have to take place or some of them will go to the wall.

There is, indeed, plenty of talk at present of Our Boys and East End joining forces for the future. Of the county clubs, Arbroath (who opposed professionalism, but who will probably have to cave in with their neighbours), Montrose, and Forfar Athletic will all run paid shows next season".

The rumours regarding the amalgamation of Our Boys and East End were confirmed when the local press reported on 15th May that negotiations with a view to merging the two clubs were at an advanced stage.

The report went on to state that: *"The feeling at present letween the Committees, players and general members of these two clubs is of the most friendly description"*, which more or less indicated that there would be little or no objection to the proposal from within both camps.

A week later, the 'Scottish Referee' reported that the terms of amalgamation had now been drawn up by joint committees, and would shortly be submitted to the clubs for approval. The amalgamation of Our Boys and East End was finalised just a few days later, and Dundee Football Club was born.

The new club wasted no time in applying for membership of the Scottish League, and at the league's Annual General Meeting, held in Glasgow on the evening of Monday 12th June 1893, their application was considered.

A total of seven clubs were in contention for the three available places; namely Renton, Abercorn and Clyde, the three clubs who had occupied the bottom three places in the Scottish League table at the end of the previous season; along with new applicants Dundee, Cowlairs, St. Bernard's and Hibernian. The merits of each club were then considered and, after much debate, the successful clubs were announced as Dundee, Renton and St. Bernard's. One of the deciding factors in Dundee's favour was that it was thought their admission would result in a great improvement, from the spectator's point of view, on the *"dreary, monotonous round of local fixtures"* that had previously been endured by the league clubs!

The unsuccesful clubs; Cowlairs, Hibernian, Clyde and Abercorn, all became members of the newly formed Second Division.

Scottish League football was coming to Dundee, and over the course of the following season local followers of the game would be able to enjoy visits to the city from clubs the calibre of Rangers, Celtic, Hearts, Dumbarton, St. Mirren, Renton, Third Lanark, Leith Athletic and St. Bernard's.

The club also entered into negotitions with the Dundee Harbour Trustees for the use of Carolina Port as their home ground. This seemed, initially, to be a foregone conclusion, as East End had occupied the ground for the previous two seasons.

With Dundee F.C. offering £100 for the forthcoming season, an increase of £20 on what had been paid previously, it seemed as if nothing could stand in their way. However, the new club was in for a shock!

Strathmore, who had once again become firmly established in the Dundee football scene, reckoned that they were now good enough to turn professional. This rather ambitious move would obviously require a football ground worthy of such a status, and Strathmore duly applied for the tenancy of Carolina Port. To make absolutely sure their application was accepted by the Harbour Trustees, Strathmore offered an incredible £150 for an eight-month lease, and naturally their offer was accepted.

With around four weeks to go before their first league fixture, Dundee F.C. were now left with a major headache, being faced with the daunting task of finding a new home ground capable of hosting Scottish League matches.

One possible option was to play at West Craigie Park, but at this time the ground was due to be taken over by a local building firm with a view to constructing new tenements similar to those which had been built over East End's former home, Pitkerro Park. Another problem regarding West Craigie Park was that it had no grandstand following the devastating fire earlier in the year.

However, it soon became apparent that setting up home at West Craigie Park, albeit on a temporary basis, was the the only solution to the problem, and Dundee F.C. successfully negotiated a short-term lease on Our Boys' former home ground.

With little time to spare, workmen were brought in to increase the level of the banking, and an application was made to and approved by the local authorities for the erection of a grandstand capable of seating 1,000 spectators.

When the league fixtures for the new season were announced, it was clear that both Dundee F.C. and the newly-improved West Craigie Park were in for the stiffest possible initiation, with Glasgow Rangers scheduled to visit Dundee for the opening match on 12th August followed by Glasgow Celtic just a week later.

There was growing excitement in local football circles in the weeks leading up to Dundee Football Club's debut in the Scottish League, and on the Wednesday preceding their opening league fixture the new club played their first ever match, a friendly against Harp at East Dock Street in front of 3,000 spectators, which ended in a draw of three goals apiece.

On Saturday 12th August, the big day finally arrived, and a huge crowd assembled in sweltering heat at West Craigie Park to witness the first-ever Scottish League match to be played in the city. With the scheduled kick-off time approaching, the Dundee players, wearing the light blue and white striped jerseys that had previously been the colours of East End, entered the field *"to a ringing cheer"*. Rangers then entered the field, and they too were received with a warm round of applause.

The visitors kicked off towards the south goal, and during the opening exchanges Dundee appeared to be over cautious, keeping posession of the ball for too long. Rangers, with the slope to their advantage, created the first opening, and home 'keeper Bill McKie had to be at his best to keep the score sheet blank. Eventually, Dundee shook off their early nerves and, after coming close on a couple of occasions, appeared to have scored when Sandy Keillor, signed from Montrose on the eve of the match, beat the Rangers 'keeper, but was ruled offside.

The first Dundee F.C. team, pictured wearing the light-blue and white stripes of East End, just before facing Rangers at West Craigie Park on 12th August 1893.

Rangers immediately broke away, and following slack defensive play from the home side, broke the deadlock with a 'soft' goal. The visitors were now playing with confidence, and less than five minutes later added a second.

At that stage it looked like the Glasgow side were about to capitalise on Dundee's inexperience and put the game beyond doubt before half-time.

The home side refused to lie down, however, and after forward Sandy Gilligan had come close, the same player headed home Dundee's first-ever league goal. The cheers of the supporters had barely died down when Rangers raced down the park and restored their two-goal advantage before half-time.

Playing downhill during the second half, the home side had the Rangers goal under pressure from the re-start, with a fierce Gilligan effort coming back off the post as confidence grew.

It was only a matter of time before they made their pressure count, and Keillor eventually reduced the leeway following good work in midfield. Roared on by the crowd, Dundee pressed hard; and, following a determined surge by all five forwards towards the Rangers goal, centre-forward Jimmy Dundas fired the ball home for the equaliser.

The spectators were now *"frantic with excitement"* as Dundee went looking for the winner, but the final whistle sounded with the score still level at three goals apiece.

It had been a tremendous display by the new club, and one of which they could be justifiably proud, but failure to convert chances had undoubtedly cost Dundee a famous victory over the club who had finished runners-up in the previous season's Scottish League championship.

A week later, an even tougher test awaited Dundee, when reigning champions Celtic visited West Craigie Park. Again, a huge crowd paid to see the action, with an estimated 9,000 inside the enclosure for what was billed as *"one of the biggest football events ever fulfilled in Dundee"*.

Dundee put on a brave performance against the league champions, and even the 'Glasgow Evening Post' was forced to admit that, *"during the whole of the first half the home team unquestionably had the best of the game"*. Failure to convert chances into goals was again the weakness of the Dundee side, however, and Celtic's experience and skill eventually came to the fore, resulting in a 4-1 victory for the Glasgow side.

The first-ever league victory was recorded on the following Saturday when Renton, the self-proclaimed 'Champions of the World', were beaten 3-2 on their own soil; a result that moved Dundee up to fourth in the league table.

Results during the first half of the league campaign proved to be disappointing on the whole, however, and by the end of the year only four wins had been recorded, along with seven defeats and two draws.

The club was also knocked out of the Scottish Cup during the first half of the season, but the circumstances surrounding their exit from the national competition were rather controversial.

The format for the tournament that season was that four qualifying rounds were to be played before the first round proper, which was scheduled for Saturday 25th November. All clubs entered into the competition were included in the draw for the first qualifying round, apart from, it would appear, the sides who had been Scottish League members during the previous season.

Dundee, therefore, were included in the first qualifying round draw for clubs from the Forfarshire Association, but when their name came out of the hat they found they had been paired with the now defunct East End.

In addition, the draw stated that Our Boys had been given a 'bye' into the second qualifying round!

The Dundee Courier, who had been wired the result of the draw from the Scottish League headquarters on the evening of Tuesday 22nd August, commented: *"No explanation is given in the telegram as to the obvious mistake in failing to recognise the amalgamation of the East End and Our Boys."*.

The obvious solution to the administrative error was to allow Dundee a 'bye' into the second round, where they were drawn to face Strathmore at Carolina Port on Saturday 23rd September. This, however, posed a huge problem, as Dundee were due to face St. Mirren in a Scottish League match on that same afternoon!

The club had no other option but to field their recognised first eleven against St. Mirren, and a second string against Strathmore; and, not surprisingly, Dundee's second eleven lost the Scottish Cup tie, and exited the tournament.

There is a further twist to the tale, however. St Bernard's, who had been admitted to the Scottish League at the same time as Dundee, were not required to play in the qualifying stages.

Is it possible that Dundee should also have bypassed the early rounds, and that their inclusion was down to the same administrative error that had initially included East End and Our Boys in the draw? If this is the case, then it would explain why the club was required to fulfil both Scottish League and Scottish Cup fixtures on the same afternoon!

There was some consolation, however, when the Forfarshire Cup was won at the first time of asking. In the final, played at Carolina Port on 20th January 1894, an incredible crowd of 10,000, (many of whom watched the match for free from an adjacent vantage point), looked on as Harp were beaten 4-0.

SCOTTISH LEAGUE 1893/94
FINAL POSITIONS

	Played	W.	L.	D.	For.	Agst.	Pts.
Celtic	18	14	3	1	53	32	29
Hearts	18	11	3	4	46	32	26
St. Bernards	18	11	6	1	53	39	23
Rangers	18	8	6	4	44	30	20
Dumbarton	18	7	6	5	32	35	19
St. Mirren	18	7	8	3	49	47	17
Third Lanark	18	7	8	3	38	44	17
Dundee	18	6	9	3	47	59	15
Leith Athletic	18	4	12	2	36	46	10
Renton	18	1	15	2	23	57	4

Goals Scored (For./Agst.)

A win counts 2 points; a draw 1 point.

The Scottish League table as it stood at the end of Dundee F.C.'s first season in the competition.

Of the five league matches still to be played by Dundee from the beginning of January 1894 to the end of the season, two were won and two were lost, with one game ending in a draw.

A somewhat disappointing final placing of eighth in the ten-team league had been attained, but the club was still in its infancy, and everyone associated with Dundee F.C. was certain that they would grow in stature as the seasons progressed.

Association football in Dundee had come a long way since that very first match, played between St. Clement's and Alexandra Athletic in Baxter Park almost two decades earlier. Few of the spectators who stood along the touch lines that cold January afternoon in 1876 would have dared predict how the game would, in future years, capture the imagination of the local population.

More to the point, even fewer could possibly have forseen that the introduction of Association football to Dundee would eventually lead to the formation of Dundee Football Club, a team who were destined to become one of the most respected and successful sides in Scotland!

Epilogue

Dundee's first season in the Scottish League turned out to be the only one played out at WestCraigiePark. Following a heated and much publicised row in November 1893 between the Northern League, Strathmore and Johnstone Wanderers, these two clubs, following much further debate and discord, decided to amalgamate under the name of Dundonians F.C. and set up home at ClepingtonPark, then the home of Johnstone Wanderers.

This move vacated the Dundee Athletic Grounds at CarolinaPort, the ground that, as mentioned in the previous chapter, Dundee F.C. had initially tried to procure shortly after their formation. During the early months of 1894, Dundee took over the lease of CarolinaPort from the Dundee Harbour Trustees, and played their first match there, a friendly against the aforementioned Dundonians, on 31st March. A few weeks later, Dundonians were re-named Dundee Wanderers, and joined the Second Division of the Scottish League. Their membership lasted only one season, however, and in 1895 they returned to the Northern League. This incarnation of Dundee Wanderers survived for several years before eventually folding in 1912.

The Northern League, which had already been weakened following the withdrawal of Our Boys and East End in May 1893, was further decimated by the resignation of Harp just a few weeks later following a row regarding admission charges. When Strathmore and Johnstone Wanderers then resigned just a few months into the following season, the competition had no other option but to go into abeyance due to a lack of member clubs. The Northern League was eventually re-started at the beginning of season 1895/96, and survived until 1920. For a number of years Dundee's reserve side was included in its membership.

Of the Dundee clubs that Our Boys and East End had regularly done battle with over the years since their foundation in the 1870's, only Lochee United survived into the 20th Century. This is not, however, the same club as the present day Lochee United. Old foes, including West End, Hibernians and Perseverance, had disappeared long before the Northern League had even been dreamt of. Harp, considered at one time to be the biggest and most formidable club in Dundee, folded in 1894, just a year after resigning from the Northern League.

Dundee remained at CarolinaPort until 1899, during which time they suffered severe financial difficulties that almost put the club out of business. There was limited success on the field of play during those very early days, but in season 1894/95 they defied the odds by reaching the semi-finals of the Scottish Cup, where they took Renton to two replays before eventually bowing out of the competition. The same stage of the tournament was reached in 1898, when Dundee went down by the odd-goal-in-five to Kilmarnock.

Following their move to DensPark during the summer of 1899, Dundee's league form gradually started to improve, and in season 1902/03 the club finished runners-up to Hibernian in the Scottish League Championship. The club also reached the semi-final of the Scottish Cup once again that season but went down to Hearts.

Dundee eventually became firmly established as serious contenders for the league title, and in season 1906/07 finished runners-up to Celtic. Two years later, that same feat was achieved, when only one point separated the same two clubs at the end of the campaign.

In season 1909/10, Dundee finally lifted their first major trophy when the Scottish Cup was won following a marathon three-match final against Clyde in April 1910.

This is, to date, the only time that the Scottish Cup has adorned the Dens Park trophy cabinet, although Dundee have been runners-up on four occasions; to Celtic in 1925, to Motherwell in 1952, and twice to Rangers in 1964 and 2003.

Apart from two seasons during the First World War, when the club withdrew from the Scottish League due to travel restrictions, Dundee maintained their top-flight status for an incredible forty-five years from 1893 until 1938, when they finished second-bottom of the table and were relegated.

Top league football eventually returned to Dundee at the end of the 1946/47 season when the club was promoted as 'B' Division champions. Two years later, Dundee once again came close to winning the Scottish League Championship, but again they were 'pipped at the post' by just one point, this time by Rangers.

In season 1951/52, Dundee did manage to win silverware once again, this time in the form of the Scottish League Cup, when Rangers were defeated by the odd-goal-in-five in a thrilling final at HampdenPark on 27th October 1951. The following season, the League Cup was brought back to DensPark for a second time after Kilmarnock were defeated at Hampden in October 1952. The League Cup was won for a third time in December 1973, following a single-goal victory over Celtic at Hampden. Dundee have been runners-up in the competition on three occasions; in 1967, 1980 and 1995.

In season 1961/62, Dundee finally won the First Division, following an epic battle with Rangers that went to the very last day of the season, when St. Johnstone were beaten 3-0 at Muirton. Winning the Scottish League meant that Dundee qualified for the 1962/63 European Cup, and the club did Scotland proud by reaching the semi-final of that prestigious competition, where they lost over two legs to eventual trophy winners Milan.

Five years later, in season 1967/68, Dundee again reached the semi-final of a European tournament, the Fairs Cup, when they went out to eventual competition winners Leeds United.

The club has also been well represented at international level over the years, and no fewer than thirty-six Dundee players have had the honour of playing for Scotland during their time with the club. There have also been several players of various different nationalities who have played for their country during their time at DensPark, including players from Argentina, Venezuela and Denmark to name but few.

In 1976, Dundee were relegated for only the second time in their history, to end another marathon stint in the top-flight of the Scottish Football League that had lasted twenty-nine years. From then until the present day Dundee has struggled to find consistency with league form, and the club has been promoted and relegated several times between the Premier League and the First Division. On four of these returns to the top-flight, Dundee were promoted as First Division Champions.

However, being members of the lower divisions gave Dundee the opportunity to compete in the Scottish League Challenge Cup, and this trophy has been won on two occasions, in 1991 and 2010.

Dundee F.C. may have had limited success during recent years, but hope springs eternal, and perhaps the great days will return to DensPark one day. The club has a history of which it can be justifiably proud, and the footballers who wore the jerseys of Our Boys and East End back in the early days of Association football in Dundee could never have dreamt that they were playing such an important part in the foundation of one of Scotland's greatest football clubs!

Sources and Bibliography

Most of the information regarding football clubs in Dundee and the surrounding area during the late nineteenth century was gained by spending many hours perusing the newspapers that are held on-line by the British Newspaper Archive. The publications most referred to via this medium were the Dundee Courier, Dundee Evening Telegraph, Dundee Advertiser and the Dundee People's Journal.

In addition, the on-line map resource held by the National Library of Scotland proved to be invaluable when working out the actual location of the many football grounds used by Dundee clubs during the late 1800's.

A number of books were also occasionally referred to; and amongst the publications perused were:

'Up Wi' The Bonnets', the Centenary History of Dundee F.C. (Norrie Price, 1993. ISBN 0952142619 (Hardback), 0952142600 (Paperback))

Across the Great Divide, a History of Professional Football in Dundee (Jim Wilkie, 1984).

The Breedon Book of Scottish Football Records (Gordon Smailes, Breedon Books, 1995. ISBN 1 85983 020 X)

Scotland: The Complete International Football Record (Richard Keir, Breedon Books, 2001. ISBN 1 85983 232 6)

If you enjoyed this book:

You might also enjoy the following publications by James K. Corstorphine, all of which are available in paperback from Amazon.co.uk:

On That Windswept Plain:
The First One Hundred Years of East Fife Football Club

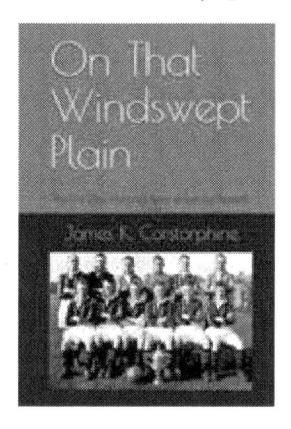

ISBN: 9781976888618

The Earliest Fife Football Clubs
Fife Football in the Late Nineteenth Century

ISBN: 9781980249580

East of Thornton Junction:
The Story of the FifeCoast Line

ISBN: 9781976909283

Dyker Lad:
Recollections of Life in an EastNeukFishingVillage

ISBN: 9781981019137

All of these titles are also available in eBook format from **Amazon.co.uk**

Printed in Poland
by Amazon Fulfillment
Poland Sp. z o.o., Wrocław